AS Biology

UNIT 2

OCR

Module 2802: Human Health and Disease

Richard Fosbery

Philip Allan Updates
Market Place
Deddington
Oxfordshire
OX15 0SE

tel: 01869 338652
fax: 01869 337590
e-mail: sales@philipallan.co.uk
www.philipallan.co.uk

This guide has been written specifically to support students preparing for the OCR AS Biology Unit 2 examination. The content has been neither approved nor endorsed by OCR and remains the sole responsibility of the author.

Printed by Information Press, Eynsham, Oxford

Contents

Introduction

■ ■ ■

Content Guidance

■ ■ ■

Questions and Answers

Introduction

About this guide

This unit guide is the second in a series of three, which cover the OCR AS specification in biology. It is intended to help you prepare for Unit 2, which examines the content of **Module 2802: Human Health and Disease**. It is divided into three sections:

- **Introduction** — this gives advice on how to use the guide to help your learning and revision and on how to prepare for the examination.
- **Content Guidance** — here you will find key facts, key concepts and links with other parts of the AS/A2 biology course; you should find the links useful in your practical work and in preparing for the other units.
- **Questions and Answers** — here there are eight questions on the topics that make up Module 2802, together with answers written by two candidates and examiner's comments.

This is not just a revision aid. This is a guide to the whole unit and you can use it throughout the 2 years of your course if you decide to go on to A2.

The Content Guidance section will help you to:

- organise your notes and check that you have highlighted the important points (key facts) — little 'chunks' of knowledge that you can remember
- understand how these 'little chunks' fit into the wider picture of biology; this will help:
  - to support Modules 2801 and 2803/01; your knowledge of the other two modules will help you understand much of the content of this one
  - to support the A2 modules, if you decide to continue the course

The Question and Answer section will help you to:

- check the way examiners ask questions at AS
- understand what the examiners' command terms mean
- interpret the question material, especially any data that the examiners give you
- write concisely and answer the questions that the examiners set

AS biology

The diagram below shows the three units that make up the AS course.

2801	2802	2803 Transport/Experimental Skills	
Biology Foundation	Human Health and Disease	Transport 2803/01 +	Coursework 2803/02 *or* Practical Examination 2803/03
30% of AS	*30% of AS*	*20% of AS*	*20% of AS*

The specification outlines what you are expected to learn and do. The content of the specification is written as **learning outcomes**; these state what you should be able to do after studying and revising each topic. Some learning outcomes are very precise and cover just a small amount of factual information. Others are much broader. Do not think that any two learning outcomes will take exactly the same length of time to cover in class or during revision. It is a good idea to write a glossary to the words in the learning outcomes; the examiners will expect you to know what they mean. This guide should help you to do this.

The unit test

The paper will be printed in a booklet, in which you will write all your answers. The paper will have five or six questions, each divided into parts. These parts comprise several short-answer questions (no more than 4 or 5 marks each) and one question requiring an extended answer, for no more than 10 marks. In the extended-answer question, 1 mark is awarded for quality of written communication (QWC). This is used to reward spelling, grammar, punctuation, legibility, organisation of ideas and use of specialist terms. The unit test has a total of 60 marks and lasts 60 minutes.

Command terms

You need to know how to respond to the various command terms used in the unit test. These are outlined below.

'Describe' and 'explain'
These do not mean the same thing! 'Describe' means give a straightforward account. You may be asked to describe something on the paper, such as a graph. You may have to describe a structure or 'tell a story', for example by writing out the sequence of events in the immune response. 'Explain' means give some *reasons* why something happens.

'Name', 'identify' and 'state'
These all require a concise answer, maybe just one word, a phrase or a sentence.

'Calculate' and 'determine'
Expect to be tested on your numeracy skills. The examiner may ask you to calculate a percentage or a mean value for a set of figures. 'Determine' means more than just calculate. You may be asked how to find a percentage change in death rates from some given data. This means that you have to select the appropriate numbers *and* do a calculation.

'Outline'
This means give several different points about the topic without concentrating on one or giving a lot of detail.

'Draw', 'sketch' and 'complete'

'Draw' and 'sketch' mean draw something on the examination paper, such as a graph, drawing or diagram. 'Complete' means that there is something that you need to finish, like a table, diagram or graph.

'Discuss'

Be prepared to write an extended answer. You will be expected to give different aspects of the topic, such as advantages and disadvantages.

'Credit will be given for using the data'

You should look at the figure or table and use some of the information in your answer. You may do this by quoting figures (with their units) or by identifying a trend and using the information to illustrate the trend you have described.

'Differences'

If you are asked to give some differences, then it is likely that you will be asked to say how 'A differs from B'. The examiners will assume that anything you write will be something about A that is not the same as for B. Sometimes there will be a table to complete to show differences.

Prepare yourself

Make sure that you have two or more blue or black pens, a couple of sharp pencils (preferably HB), a ruler, an eraser, a pencil sharpener, a watch and a calculator.

When told to start the paper, look through all the questions. Find the end of the last question (it may be on the back page — don't miss it). Find and read the question that requires an extended answer. Some points may come to mind immediately — write them down before you forget.

There is no need to start by answering question 1, but the examiner will have set something quite straightforward to help calm your nerves. Look carefully at the number of marks available for each question. Do not write a lengthy answer if there are only 1 or 2 marks available. If you want to change an answer, then cross it out and rewrite the answer clearly. If you write an answer or continue an answer somewhere other than on the allotted lines, then indicate clearly where this is.

When you reach the question that requires an extended answer:
- plan what you intend to write and make sure it is in a logical sequence
- do not write out the question
- keep to the point — you do not need an introduction or a summary
- use bullet points if they help your answer
- pay careful attention to spelling, punctuation and grammar

Time yourself. Work out where you expect to be after 30 minutes (half time). Leave yourself at least 5 minutes to check your paper to make sure you have attempted all the questions and have left nothing out. The best way to do this is to check the mark allocation — have you offered something for each mark?

Content Guidance

The Content Guidance section is a guide to the content of Module 2802: Human Health and Disease. The main areas of this module are:

- Introduction to health and disease
- Diet
- Gaseous exchange and exercise
- Smoking and disease
- Infectious diseases
- Immunity

This section will help you to organise your notes and highlight the important points. The 'key facts' are presented as easy-to-remember chunks of knowledge. This section will also help you to understand the links with other parts of the AS and A2 course, including practical work.

Units

Various units are used in this module. This is just to remind you.

Volume: cm^3 and dm^3; $1000\,cm^3 = 1\,dm^3$

You will often find ml (millilitre) on glassware and in books. Examination papers, however, use cm^3 (cubic centimetre or 'centimetre cubed') and dm^3 (cubic decimetre or 'decimetre cubed'). $1\,cm^3 = 1\,ml$; $1\,dm^3 = 1$ litre (1l or 1L).

In this module you will come across volumes in the section on gaseous exchange and exercise with such measurements as tidal volume, vital capacity, stroke volume and cardiac output.

Length: nm, μm, mm, m and km; 1000 nm (nanometres) = 1 μm (micrometre); 1000 μm = 1 mm (millimetre); 1000 mm = 1 m; 1000 m = 1 km

In this module, you may be expected to find the measurements or magnifications of cells, such as white blood cells in the section on immunity, or cells in the lining of the gaseous exchange system. Data on exercise physiology may include distances (m or km) run by athletes or their speed (given as $m\,s^{-1}$, which means metres per second, or $km\,h^{-1}$, which means kilometres per hour).

Pressure: Pa (pascals) and kPa (kilopascals); 1000 Pa = 1 kPa

The medical profession uses mmHg (millimetres of mercury) for measuring blood pressure. Examination papers use kilopascals. 'Normal' blood pressure is often given as '120 over 80' or 120 mmHg (systolic) and 80 mmHg (diastolic). These are equivalent to 15.8 kPa and 10.5 kPa. See page 25 for more about this.

Energy: joules (J), kilojoules (kJ) and megajoules (MJ); 1000 J = 1 kJ, 1000 kJ = 1 MJ

The energy provided by your diet is given in kilojoules (or in megajoules). On packets of food and in books on diet you will often find energy as calories or kilocalories. These units are not used in examination papers.

content guidance

Introduction to health and disease

Defining health and disease

Key concepts you must understand

Most of the topics in this module concern disease rather than health. Both the terms 'health' and 'disease' are difficult to define, and you should be aware of this. However, here are some simple definitions:

- Health is physical, mental and social well-being. It is more than just being free from disease.
- Disease is a malfunction of the mind or body leading to a condition of poor health.

People who consider themselves 'healthy' because they are not suffering from the symptoms of a disease may have low physical fitness and may be developing a serious condition, such as heart disease or lung cancer.

Key facts you must know

There are many different illnesses and diseases that we might suffer from. In this module, these are classified into the nine different categories outlined in Figure 1.

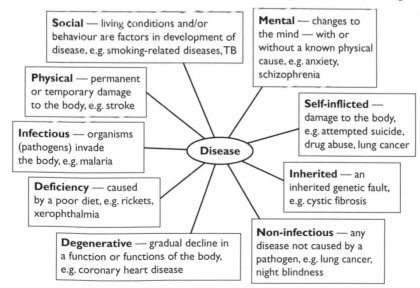

Social — living conditions and/or behaviour are factors in development of disease, e.g. smoking-related diseases, TB

Mental — changes to the mind — with or without a known physical cause, e.g. anxiety, schizophrenia

Physical — permanent or temporary damage to the body, e.g. stroke

Self-inflicted — damage to the body, e.g. attempted suicide, drug abuse, lung cancer

Infectious — organisms (pathogens) invade the body, e.g. malaria

Disease

Deficiency — caused by a poor diet, e.g. rickets, xerophthalmia

Inherited — an inherited genetic fault, e.g. cystic fibrosis

Degenerative — gradual decline in a function or functions of the body, e.g. coronary heart disease

Non-infectious — any disease not caused by a pathogen, e.g. lung cancer, night blindness

Figure 1 Nine categories of disease

The choice of categories is arbitrary — there are many other categories that we could have chosen, such as occupational diseases or those affecting named parts of the body, for example cardiovascular diseases (which affect the heart and circulatory system). Figure 1 shows how these categories relate to one another. Many diseases can be placed into more than one category. You should know one example from each category.

Epidemiology

Key concepts you must understand

Epidemiology is the study of patterns of diseases. It is concerned with what categories of people catch infectious diseases and develop non-infectious diseases. Epidemiologists find out the factors that these people have in common, so they can try to identify the causes and the people who are at risk of developing the same diseases.

Standards of health vary within a country and between different countries. Collecting statistics on health is important in finding out how these patterns of health and disease vary in different countries or between different groups of people, and how they change over time.

Key facts you must know

You should learn the following three terms that refer to diseases:
- **epidemic** — an outbreak of disease in a population
- **pandemic** — an outbreak of disease that occurs across the world or across continents
- **endemic** — this describes diseases that are *always* in a population

Epidemiologists collect different types of data on diseases. Three examples are:
- **incidence** — how many people fall ill (or are diagnosed) with a disease over a certain period of time, such as a week, a month or a year (e.g. the number who catch influenza during one week)
- **prevalence** — the number of people who have a disease during a period of time (e.g. the total number who had asthma in 2001)
- **mortality** — the number of people who died during a period of time (e.g. the number who died from lung cancer in 2001)

Epidemiologists collect data to show how these patterns change. The aims of collecting data are to:
- make comparisons between populations at the same time, for example Scotland and England
- make comparisons between populations at different times, for example now and 10 years ago
- find out which diseases are important
- find new, emerging diseases, such as SARS (severe acute respiratory syndrome)
- inform policy-making about providing resources in the health service
- find out how well government health policies are working
- investigate the spread of disease and investigate the likely causes

The data collected by health statisticians are adjusted so that valid comparisons can be made. Table 1 shows mortality data for the four countries of the UK. Often, such data are given as *deaths per 100 000 of the population*. The figures in Table 1 have been converted into this form and appear in *italics*.

Country	All causes	Lung cancer	Coronary heart disease	Stroke	Respiratory diseases, e.g. bronchitis	Population/ millions
England	503 026	27 176	101 163	49 059	87 956	49.1
	1024	*55*	*206*	*100*	*179*	
Wales	33 501	1718	7228	3335	5909	2.9
	1155	*59*	*249*	*115*	*204*	
Scotland	57 799	3948	12 412	6803	6547	5.1
	1133	*77*	*243*	*133*	*128*	
Northern Ireland	14 903	792	3234	1469	3019	1.7
	877	*47*	*190*	*86*	*178*	
UK	**609 229**	**33 634**	**124 037**	**60 666**	**103 431**	**58.8**
	1036	*57*	*211*	*103*	*176*	

Table 1 Deaths from main causes and all causes for people of all ages in the UK (2000); figures in italics are deaths per 100 000 of the population

Deaths rates from coronary heart disease for men under 65 in different areas of England are shown in Figure 2.

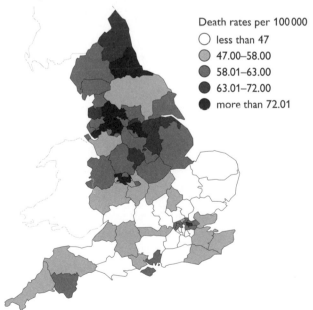

Death rates per 100 000
○ less than 47
● 47.00–58.00
● 58.01–63.00
● 63.01–72.00
● more than 72.01

Figure 2 Death rates from CHD for men under 65 in different areas in England

Standards of health differ widely between less economically developed and more economically developed counties. Table 2 shows some of the ways in which the health of different countries can be compared.

Indicator of health	UK	The Gambia
Total population/millions	58.8	1.3
Population density/people per km²	58830	1305
Life expectancy of males, *females*/years	75.2, *80.1*	52.0, *56.0*
Total fertility rate/children per woman of childbearing age	1.7	5.61
Birth rate/births per thousand	12	41.25
Infant mortality/deaths per thousand live births	5.6	76.39
Death rate/deaths per thousand per year	10.2	12.63
Average population growth/% per year	0.18	3.3
% of children vaccinated against measles	95	91
Number of doctors, *nurses* per 100 000 population	3.5, *12.5*	170, *710*

Table 2 Some different ways of comparing health in the UK and in The Gambia (a less economically developed country in West Africa)

More economically developed countries have low rates of infectious diseases but the rates of long-term degenerative diseases are high. In less economically developed countries, the opposite is the case. This is an oversimplification, of course, but it is worth remembering this if you are given data about standards of health in different countries.

Table 1 shows that although the number of deaths in Wales is much less than in England, the death rates (per 100 000) are broadly similar. The table shows that more deaths occur from coronary heart disease than any other disease. Figure 2 shows that the highest death rates from coronary heart disease among men under 65 occur in large urban areas, such as Manchester, Liverpool and Newcastle.

The Human Genome Project

Key concepts you must understand

The genome is the sum of all the genes that we have. There are about 30 000 of these and we now know where they are on the chromosomes. The Human Genome Project (HGP) involved locating the genes on chromosomes and then 'decoding' them as sequences of nucleotide bases (A, T, C and G — see Figure 3). Here it would be good to check the section on genetic control of protein synthesis in Module 2801 to remind yourself about the triplets (e.g. AAA) and the way in which they code for the amino acids that are assembled to make proteins.

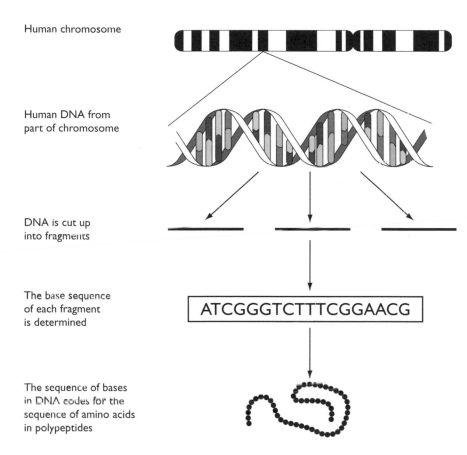

Human chromosome

Human DNA from part of chromosome

DNA is cut up into fragments

The base sequence of each fragment is determined

ATCGGGTCTTTCGGAACG

The sequence of bases in DNA codes for the sequence of amino acids in polypeptides

Figure 3 The Human Genome Project has identified the base sequences in human genes

Key facts you must know

Some of the advantages for health of the HGP are:

- Genetic tests have been developed for inherited diseases, such as cystic fibrosis. More of these will be developed now that the sequences of the genes are known.
- Tests have also been developed to find out whether people have inherited alleles of genes that increase the likelihood that they will develop diseases such as breast cancer and Alzheimer's.
- Doctors will be able to diagnose diseases more accurately and choose more appropriate treatments, avoiding drugs likely to have side effects.
- Gene therapy may be carried out to insert properly functioning alleles. This has already happened to treat a rare immunodeficiency disease.
- Pharmaceutical companies may be able to develop drugs better able to target specific problems.
- Medical researchers will have more data when looking for causes of disease and finding cures.

Links The Human Genome Project has 'decoded' all the human genes. Module 2801 has a section about genetic control of protein synthesis. Revise this to ensure that you can *explain* that, by knowing the genetic code, it is possible to predict the primary structure of a protein and hence its overall structure and its role in the body. Note, however, that not all human genes are transcribed and translated, and the sequence of bases that is transcribed as RNA is cut before being released from the nucleus to the cytoplasm. There is much that we have yet to discover about what genes do and how they interact during our development. You should know about mutation from GCSE. Mutation causes DNA sequences to change and it is these *changed* sequences that are responsible for inherited diseases. You will learn more about this in the A2 Module 2804 (Central Concepts) where you will also study the implications of the HGP, which involves more than just consequences for human health.

Diet

The concept of a balanced diet

Key concepts you must understand

A balanced diet must provide us with:
- sufficient energy for our needs
- nutrients for many functions, including making compounds required in cells, tissues and organs:
  - essential amino acids (EAAs)
  - essential fatty acids (EFAs)
  - vitamins
  - minerals
- sufficient water to replace losses
- fibre

Carbohydrates, fats and proteins provide the energy in our diet. These compounds are the fuels for cells that transfer energy to ATP — the common currency of energy in cells. This occurs in respiration.

An unbalanced diet leads to malnutrition. A diet deficient in energy may cause starvation, weight loss, poor growth, and can eventually prove fatal. A diet that provides too much energy for a person's needs may lead to obesity.

Figure 4 is an important concept to understand at this stage. If we investigate how much energy people of the same age and gender require every day, we obtain this normal distribution curve (or bell-shaped curve). This shows that most individuals require near the average for the group, but there are some who need more energy than this and others who need less. Exactly the same distribution is obtained for intakes of the different nutrients. This idea of the normal distribution is central to understanding **dietary reference values** (see pages 16–18). Figure 5 shows recommended energy intakes for people of different ages.

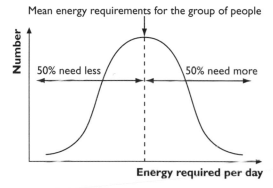

Mean energy requirements for the group of people

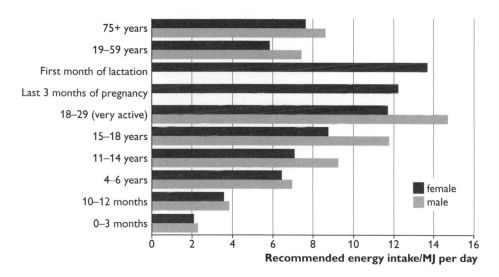

Figure 4 A normal distribution curve for energy intake for a sample of people of the same gender and age

Figure 5 Recommendations for energy intake

Key facts you must know

Table 3 on page 16 shows some of the nutrients that we need in our diet, their roles in the body and what happens if there is a deficiency.

In addition, we also need:
- fibre, which passes straight through the gut because it is not digested; it helps prevent constipation
- water, to replace the amount lost in breath, sweat etc. — water is the solvent in the blood plasma and tissue fluid; it takes part in hydrolysis reactions during digestion and helps us lose heat to our surroundings as sweat

Nutrient	Role in the body	Effect of deficiency
Essential amino acids (EAAs)	Used to make proteins (These are the amino acids that we cannot synthesise ourselves; we do not have the enzymes to make them from anything else, so they have to be in the diet)	Poor growth (Deficiency is unlikely in the UK as most proteins in the national diet contain all the EAAs)
Essential fatty acids (EFAs)	Used to make phospholipids and fats (These are the fatty acids that we cannot synthesise since we do not have the enzymes for making them)	Poor growth (Deficiency is most unlikely)
Vitamin A	Used to make rhodopsin for functioning of rod cells in the eye Used to make retinoic acid, which aids cell development and growth, especially in epithelia	Dry, rough skin and xerophthalmia or drying of the cornea Night blindness — cannot detect light when the light is dim or of low intensity
Vitamin D	A steroid hormone that controls absorption of calcium from the gut and its deposition in bones (Made in the skin from another molecule when exposed to sunlight)	Children — rickets Adults — osteomalacia Softening and weakening of the bones, because calcium is not deposited
Iron	Used to make haem in haemoglobin for carrying oxygen	Iron-deficiency anaemia (There are other sorts of anaemia with different causes)
Calcium	To make hard material in bones and teeth	Stunted growth Osteoporosis Softening of bones

Table 3

Dietary reference values (DRVs)

How much food should we eat? If you look at packets of food, you will often find the recommended daily allowances (RDAs) for nutrients. This is one set of recommendations for adults. In 1991, the UK government published a report that made recommendations for males and females of different ages, taking into consideration the range of requirements within each age group. It also made recommendations for women during pregnancy and lactation (breast feeding).

For most nutrients, there are three DRVs:
- **Estimated Average Requirement (EAR)** — this is the population average
- **Reference Nutrient Intake (RNI)** — this is at the top end of the range and is enough for about 97% of the population
- **Lower Reference Nutrient Intake (LRNI)** — this is at the bottom of the range and is enough for only about 2% of the population

The DRV for energy is the EAR. This is because our energy requirements vary and if everyone were to consume the amount of food required by those with very high energy needs, for example very active people, then many would become overweight or obese. If people consume slightly more minerals and vitamins than they really need, they are unlikely to come to any harm. However, consuming even slightly more energy than you need each day increases the risk of becoming overweight or obese. The EAR tells us the *average* requirement for our age group.

There were not enough data available to set reference values for some nutrients and the DRV for these, for example fluoride, is the **Safe Intake**, which is enough to meet our needs but not enough to be harmful.

The DRVs for carbohydrate and fat are set as percentages of energy intake. These are:
- total fat — no more than 33–35%, of which
  - saturated fat — no more than 10%
  - EFAs — linoleic acid 1.0%, linolenic acid 0.2%
- carbohydrates
  - starch — no more than 37–39%
  - sugars, e.g. sucrose — no more than 10%

Table 4 shows the DRVs for some important nutrients in young adults. You should remember that the DRVs are for groups of people in the UK. They do not tell you whether you (as an individual) are obtaining sufficient energy and nutrients. However, if your diet provides you with the RNI for nutrients, then you are likely to be receiving enough. Only 2.28% of people with very high requirements need more. Dieticians use DRVs to plan diets for the military, schools and hospitals. Nutritional scientists who carry out surveys of our eating habits also use them, for example when studying the effects of people's income on their diet and health. DRVs are used when working with *groups* of people.

Nutrient	Male	Female	Pregnancy	Lactation (first month)
Protein/g day^{-1}	55.2	45.0	+ 6.0	+ 11.0
Vitamin A/µg day^{-1}	700	600	+ 100	+ 350
Vitamin D/µg day^{-1}	0	0	+ 10	+ 10
Calcium/mg day^{-1}	1000	800	–	+ 550
Iron/mg day^{-1}	11.3	14.8	–	–
Folic acid/µg day^{-1}	200	200	+ 100	+ 60
Fluoride/mg per kg body mass day^{-1}	0.05	0.05	–	–
Fibre/g day^{-1}	18	18	–	–

Table 4 Dietary reference values for young adults. The figures for pregnancy and lactation should be added to the figures given for females. The nutrients are RNIs, except for fluoride for which there is only a Safe Intake.

Figure 6 shows the DRVs for iron for young adults. This shows that the RNI provides sufficient for 97% of the population, the LRNI for only 2.28%. The DRVs for females at this age are higher than those for males because females lose blood at menstruation and a greater intake of iron is necessary to make up for this loss. If individuals consume less than the RNI, they may be at risk of anaemia. If they consume only slightly less, then there may not be a problem. However, if they consume *significantly* less than the RNI, there is a greater risk of developing anaemia.

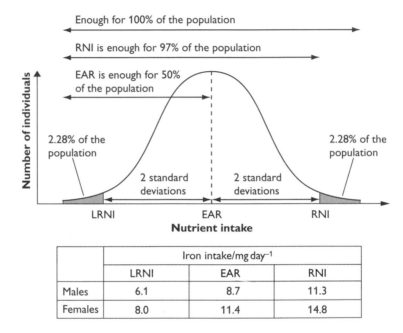

	Iron intake/mg day^{-1}		
	LRNI	EAR	RNI
Males	6.1	8.7	11.3
Females	8.0	11.4	14.8

Figure 6 Dietary reference values for iron for young adults. You may know about standard deviation (SD), which is a way of measuring the spread of results about the mean. The RNI is set as two standard deviations above the mean and the LRNI as two standard deviations below the mean.

You are not expected to remember individual DRVs for specific nutrients, but you should be able to interpret information about DRVs for major nutrients that we require in our diet and explain why we need these nutrients. You should be able to explain that there are higher DRVs for pregnancy and lactation to provide energy and nutrients to support the growth of the fetus and, later, for the child.

Malnutrition

Not enough food

Kwashiorkor and marasmus are two extreme forms of **protein energy malnutrition** (PEM) commonly seen in young children who do not receive enough food. The protein in their diet gets used for energy. Children with kwashiorkor appear bloated; those with marasmus are thin and emaciated. If the energy content of the diet is increased, then protein is spared and used for growth, repair and maintenance. What children like this need is usually an increase in their energy intake with only a little extra protein in their diet, if any. But the diet must contain all the essential amino acids (EAAs). If these children receive supplementary feeding (e.g. during a famine or in a refugee camp), then their diet must contain all of these EAAs.

Kwashiorkor and marasmus are two ways in which children respond to PEM and it is difficult to know whether a child will develop one form or the other during starvation. It is thought that children with marasmus are adapting to PEM better than those with kwashiorkor.

Anorexia nervosa is a form of marasmus, but brought on to a large extent by psychological factors. There are many problems that result, including muscle loss, emaciation and limited sexual development.

Too much food

If a person's body mass is 20% or more above the recommended mass for height, then that person is obese. The energy intake has far exceeded the energy consumption and the excess has been stored as fat. Obese people are at risk from a variety of diseases such as diabetes, arthritis and coronary heart disease. (There is more about this in Question 2 — see page 53.)

Diet and coronary heart disease

Coronary heart disease (CHD) is a degenerative condition that involves the build-up of fatty tissue in the walls of the arteries that supply heart muscle. If these arteries become narrowed as a result, the flow of blood decreases and the supply of nutrients and oxygen to the heart muscle decreases. The muscle does not release enough energy and the heart becomes weak. There may be a blood clot in the coronary artery, so cutting off the supply of blood to that area completely and leading to a heart attack. There are many factors that influence the development of fatty tissue in the coronary arteries; some involve the diet.

One of the risk factors in CHD is the cholesterol concentration in the blood. This increases if the diet is rich in saturated fat. Foods such as meat, butter, whole-fat milk and cheese are rich in saturated fat and tend to raise blood cholesterol. Polyunsaturated fats in foods such as oily fish tend to have the opposite effect. Cholesterol in the diet has a small effect on increasing blood cholesterol. Individuals concerned about their blood cholesterol are advised to avoid foods rich in saturated fat and cholesterol. Antioxidants, such as vitamins C and E, are protective in that they help to reduce the chances of developing CHD. Fresh fruit and vegetables are rich sources and should be included in the diet.

Links There are numerous links with Module 2801 in this section. You should have a look at the following:

- the structure of glucose and starch — starch is an important source of energy in our diet
- the structure of cellulose, which provides much of the fibre in the diet
- the structure of saturated and unsaturated fats
- protein structure
- the roles of water in living organisms
- the ions that are relevant here — calcium, phosphate, iron, chloride, sodium, potassium and magnesium

Figures 4 and 6 are normal distribution curves. EAR is the mean for the age group; RNI and LRNI are set two standard deviations above and below the mean, respectively. Standard deviation (SD) is a useful concept to know in biology, especially when you are analysing your results in coursework or you are asked to comment on results in an examination question.

Try classifying anorexia nervosa into the categories of disease in Figure 1 on page 9. Can you think of reasons for classifying it in all of the categories *except* 'inherited' and 'infectious'?

Gaseous exchange and exercise

The gaseous exchange system

Key concepts you must understand

Figure 7 shows the structure of the gaseous exchange system, consisting of the trachea and lungs.

You should be clear about three different aspects of the gaseous exchange system:
- ventilation — breathing air in and out of the lungs
- gaseous exchange — diffusion of oxygen and carbon dioxide between air in the alveoli and the blood
- respiration — chemical processes that occur inside cells to transfer energy from molecules such as glucose and fat to ATP. Respiration may be aerobic or anaerobic.

In this section, we are mainly concerned with the distribution of the cells and tissues in the trachea and lungs and their functions. You should see some microscope sections of the trachea and the lungs. For this unit, you do not need to know how the breathing movements ventilate the lungs.

This section is also about aerobic exercise and aerobic fitness. When you run, cycle, swim or take similar forms of exercise, your muscles need to be supplied with oxygen so that they can respire aerobically and not anaerobically. To do this, the heart and lungs must respond to provide them with sufficient oxygen. If muscles respire anaerobically, they produce lactate (lactic acid) and this will eventually cause you to stop exercising. Aerobic fitness develops when the heart and lungs are able to provide oxygen efficiently. In sports that involve short bursts of activity, such as sprinting and weightlifting, muscles respire anaerobically and the heart and lungs do not respond in the same way.

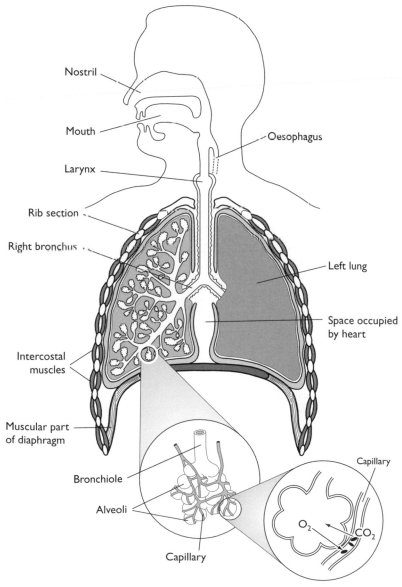

Figure 7 The gaseous exchange system, with details of the gaseous exchange surface formed by alveoli

Key facts you must know

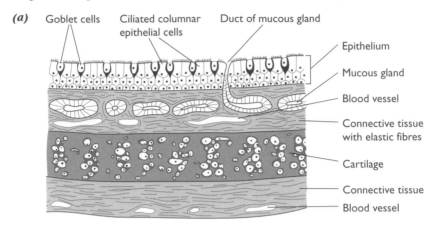

(a)
Goblet cells Ciliated columnar epithelial cells Duct of mucous gland

Epithelium
Mucous gland
Blood vessel
Connective tissue with elastic fibres
Cartilage
Connective tissue
Blood vessel

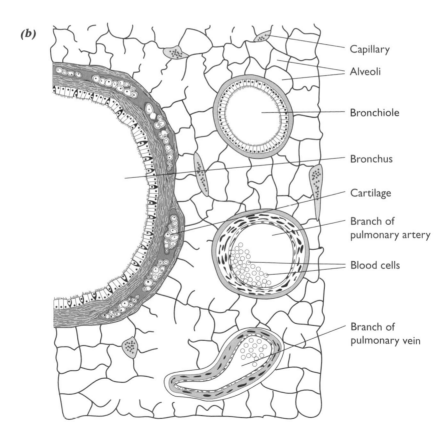

(b)
Capillary
Alveoli
Bronchiole
Bronchus
Cartilage
Branch of pulmonary artery
Blood cells
Branch of pulmonary vein

Figure 8 (a) Detail of the wall of the trachea.
(b) Distribution of tissues in the lungs.

Structure	Distribution in gaseous exchange system	Functions
Ciliated epithelium	Trachea, bronchi, bronchioles	Cilia move mucus up the airways
Goblet cells	Trachea, bronchi	Secrete mucus
Cartilage	Trachea, bronchi	Holds open the airways to allow easy flow of air
Smooth muscle	Trachea, bronchi and bronchioles	Contracts to narrow the airways
Elastic fibres	In all parts of the system, including alveoli	Stretch when breathing in; recoil when breathing out, helping to force air out of the lungs
Squamous epithelium	Alveoli	Thin, to give a short diffusion pathway for gaseous exchange Alveoli provide a large surface area
Capillaries	In all parts of the system — many around alveoli	Provide a large surface area for exchange between blood and air

Table 5 Components of the gaseous exchange system and their functions

Lung volumes

- **Tidal volume** is the volume of air that you breathe in and then breathe out during one breath. At rest it is usually about 500 cm³. It increases when you exercise, sing or play a wind instrument.
- **Vital capacity** is the volume of air you can force out after taking a deep breath. In young adult males it may be about 4.6 dm³; in females, 3.1 dm³. Athletes, singers and wind instrument players often have larger vital capacities than these.

These are two measurements of lung function. The **total lung volume** is the vital capacity plus the volume of air that is left in the lungs after you breathe out forcibly. This residual volume is usually about 1 dm³. The total lung volume of young males may therefore be between 5 dm³ and 6 dm³.

Links Gaseous exchange features in the other two AS modules. You could save yourself some time by revising the following topics together: the structure of the whole system (for this module); the arrangement of squamous and ciliated cells (for Module 2801); the diffusion of carbon dioxide and oxygen across the alveoli (for Modules 2801 and 2803/01) and the reasons for having a large surface area in the lungs (for 2803/01).

You may be asked about the trachea and the lungs in the practical examination. If you are going to take this examination, then you should study microscope slides of these two organs and be able to recognise the different tissues and cells, such as the ciliated epithelia, goblet cells, smooth muscle and cartilage. You should be able to make *outline* drawings of:

● the trachea, to show the distribution of the tissues
● the lungs, to show the bronchioles, branches of the pulmonary artery and vein, and the alveoli

When making these outline drawings, you should not draw any cells. You may be asked to draw a few cells from areas such as the lining of the airways (trachea, bronchus and bronchioles). You should always be able to identify the different cell types and describe how they are stained.

The cardiovascular system

Key concepts you must understand

The cardiovascular system is composed of the heart and blood vessels (arteries, arterioles, veins and capillaries). Remember, 'cardio-' refers to the **heart** and 'vascular' refers to the **transport system**.

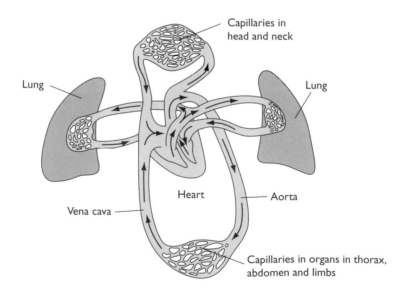

**Figure 9 Diagram of the cardiovascular system
(this is covered in more detail in Module 2803/01)**

The heart pumps deoxygenated blood to the lungs and oxygenated blood to the rest of the body. In this module, it is important to remember that the heart supplies tissues, such as muscles, with oxygen and nutrients. It responds to the body's needs, so during exercise the volume of blood pumped out with each beat increases and the heart rate increases. Breathing also changes — the depth (tidal volume) and the rate of breathing increase. This is how the heart and lungs respond to aerobic exercise. As a result of training, the response of these organs during exercise improves so that there is a better supply of oxygen and glucose to muscles.

Key facts you must know

Pulse

You can feel the pulse at pressure points in the body, such as over the artery in the wrist. Taking the pulse is a measurement of the heart rate. A low resting pulse rate is a good indicator of aerobic fitness, since it means the heart is pumping out a large volume of blood with each beat and does not need to increase its rate too much during exercise.

Blood pressure

Blood must have a pressure in order to overcome resistance of the blood vessels and flow through the circulatory system. When the heart pumps, it increases the pressure of the blood. Blood pressure is usually measured in an artery in the arm. The systolic blood pressure is the highest value recorded in the artery and diastolic blood pressure is the lowest value recorded in the artery (see Figure 10).

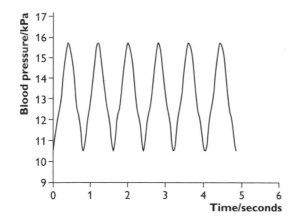

Figure 10 *The results of continuously monitoring the blood pressure in an artery in the arm. Systolic pressure is 15.8 kPa and diastolic pressure is 10.5 kPa. The pulse rate is 6 beats in 5 seconds or 72 beats per minute.*

Pulse rates and blood pressure vary during the day and from day to day. They both increase during exercise.

Hypertension (high blood pressure)

Blood pressure may increase during life. The reasons why this happens are not well understood, although being overweight or obese is certainly one of them. If a person's resting systolic blood pressure is greater than 18.7 kPa, he/she is regarded as having hypertension, which is an important risk factor in CHD (see pages 31–33). Drugs may be taken to lower blood pressure.

Aerobic exercise

Figure 11 shows the effects of exercise on some key areas of the body. Figure 12 shows what happens immediately after exercise has finished. During exercise (even aerobic exercise), some anaerobic respiration occurs. This often happens at the very beginning of exercise as it takes time for the heart and lungs to respond and supply enough oxygen to the muscles. Anaerobic respiration produces lactate (also known as lactic acid). This must be removed from the body. It is taken up by the liver and respired or converted to glucose. It builds up during an oxygen deficit when the lungs do not take in enough oxygen. At the end of exercise, there is an oxygen debt that is paid off by breathing deeply, as the athlete is doing in Figure 12.

Gaseous exchange system
- Athlete's tidal volume and breathing rate increase, so lungs supply plenty of oxygen and remove plenty of carbon dioxide

Cardiovascular system
- Athlete's heart beats harder and faster and pumps out a larger volume of blood with each beat
- Systolic blood pressure increases
- Blood flow through muscles increases to provide more glucose and oxygen

Muscular system
- Rate of aerobic respiration increases to provide more ATP for muscle contraction, so athlete can run faster and win!

Figure 11 Aerobic exercise

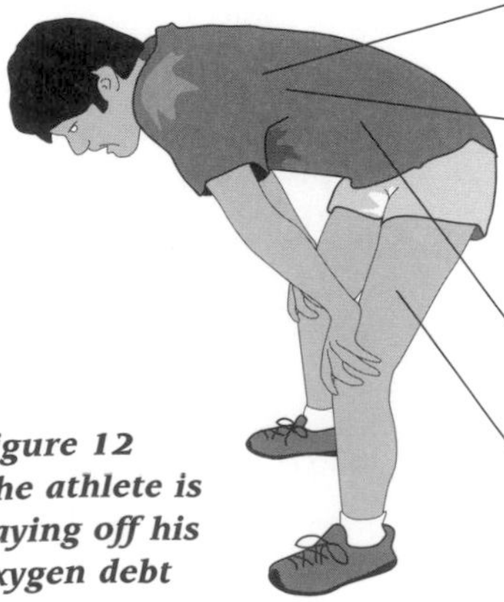

Gaseous exchange system
- Athlete continues to breathe deeply to supply oxygen and remove carbon dioxide

Cardiovascular system
- Athlete's heart continues to pump out more blood than at rest
- Systolic blood pressure decreases
- Plenty of blood continues to flow through muscles to remove carbon dioxide, lactate and heat

Liver
- Breaks down lactate to carbon dioxide and water; converts some lactate to glucose

Muscular system
- Rate of aerobic respiration decreases as less energy is required now that exercise has stopped

*Figure 12
The athlete is
paying off his
oxygen debt*

Investigating the effects of exercise on the body

Table 6 shows the results of an investigation carried out by some students.

Measurement	At rest	During strenuous exercise	During recovery
Tidal volume/dm^3	0.5	3.3	1.7
Breathing rate/breaths min^{-1}	12	24	18
Ventilation rate/dm^3 min^{-1} (volume of air breathed out in 1 minute)	6.0	80.0	30.6
Pulse rate/beats per minute	70	190	120
Systolic blood pressure/kPa	15.0	26.1	21.0
Diastolic blood pressure/kPa	10.0	10.5	10.5

Table 6

This shows the sorts of measurements that can be made before, during and after exercise. It is easiest to do this with heart and blood pressure monitors and a data logger. (It is difficult to record precise and reliable results if taking your pulse measurements during an investigation like this with fingers placed over pressure points.) It also helps if you can measure the amount of work that you do during exercise — say by using an exercise bicycle or rowing machine at a fitness centre.

You can find out how much exercise is necessary to achieve a significant improvement in aerobic fitness by taking the **resting pulse** at regular intervals during a training programme. It helps to start with someone who does not take much exercise and is not very fit. Question 5 on page 62 is an example of the sort of investigation that could be done. Remember, you should always refer to the *resting* pulse in this sort of investigation. It is also possible to measure improvements in oxygen intake during exercise, but this requires complex equipment that you are unlikely to have access to. It is possible to convert recovery pulse rates into fitness scores and into figures for oxygen consumption.

Warning

You must always carry out a risk assessment before undertaking any experimental work as part of your course. Do not undertake any investigation into exercise unless you know that the person exercising does not have a medical condition that would put them at risk.

The long-term effects of exercise on the body

Exercise is an essential part of maintaining good health. It has a number of beneficial effects on systems of the body. It is a good idea to know two or three effects for each system.

Gaseous exchange system:
- increase in vital capacity
- improved uptake of oxygen in the lungs

Cardiovascular system:
- decrease in resting heart rate
- increase in stroke volume (volume of blood pumped out of the heart with each beat)
- increase in cardiac output (volume of blood pumped out in each minute)

Muscular system:
- increase in number of mitochondria in muscle tissue
- increase in glycogen and fat stored in muscle
- more capillaries in muscle — better supply of oxygen

Rest of the body:
- strengthened ligaments, tendons and bones
- reduced cholesterol concentration in the blood

Regular aerobic exercise also helps to decrease the chances of developing diseases such as coronary heart disease.

To be of benefit, aerobic exercise should be undertaken three times a week at 70% of your age-predicted maximum heart rate, which is calculated by subtracting your age from 220. For example, if you are 17 then the heart rate during exercise should be about 142 beats per minute.

Links Much useful background information on the cardiovascular system is covered in the first two sections of Module 2803/01. It is important that you make the links between the two modules. For example, heart structure and function is covered in Module 2803/01 and the role of the heart in exercise is covered here. In explaining the role of the heart in this module, you should be prepared to write about such concepts as heart rate, blood pressure, stroke volume and cardiac output.

You may consider doing an investigation on exercise for your coursework. Unless you have access to good equipment that you can use to measure pulse rates and blood pressures, then it is unlikely that you will be able to take precise measurements. However, you could have a useful discussion with fellow students about how to carry out such an investigation, the variables you would need to control and the precautions you would take. Question 5 on page 62 will give you some ideas about how to plan such an investigation. This may provide some useful ideas for your coursework investigation on another topic in the AS course.

Smoking and disease

Key concepts you must understand

This section is about the effects of cigarette smoke on the gaseous exchange and cardiovascular systems. Make sure you know the difference between the two systems. Confusing the two loses candidates lots of marks! Smoking causes lung diseases, such as chronic bronchitis, emphysema and lung cancer. It is involved in the development of cardiovascular diseases, such as stroke and coronary heart disease. It is also implicated in many other diseases, such cancers of the mouth, oesophagus and bladder.

Key facts you must know

Cigarette smoke has over 4000 substances in it. The important constituents are:

- tar — a black oily liquid which settles in the bronchi and bronchioles
- carcinogens — cancer-causing chemicals, e.g. benzpyrene
- carbon monoxide
- nicotine — the drug in tobacco that is absorbed into the blood

Figure 13 shows the effects of tar and carcinogens on the gaseous exchange system.

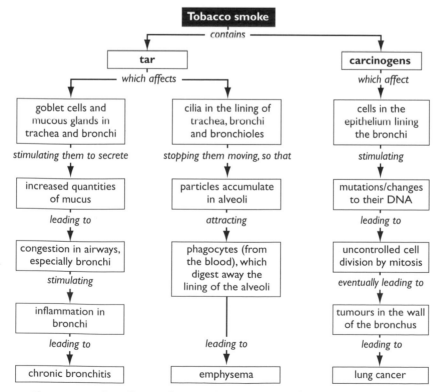

Figure 13 The effects of tar and carcinogens from tobacco smoke on the gaseous exchange system

Long-term smoking causes progressive changes in the linings of the airways, particularly in the bronchi. Figure 14 shows the changes that occur in chronic bronchitis. Emphysema occurs when the walls of the alveoli are broken down by white blood cells that invade the air spaces to destroy bacteria and particles that have been carried by the air and not removed by the mucus and cilia in the bronchi and bronchioles. Figure 15 shows the difference between the pattern of alveoli in the lung of a non-smoker and that of a smoker with emphysema.

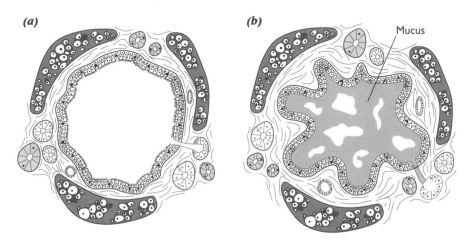

Figure 14 Cross-section of a bronchus of (a) a non-smoker and (b) a smoker. The smoker has bronchitis.

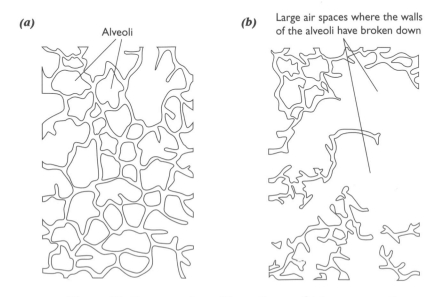

Figure 15 Cross-section of lung tissue of (a) a non-smoker and (b) a smoker. The smoker has emphysema.

Evidence linking smoking with lung cancer

There are two lines of evidence:
- epidemiological
- experimental

Epidemiology is the study of patterns of disease. Lung cancer was a rare disease in the nineteenth century. It began to increase in the UK in the early decades of the twentieth century and by the 1950s there was an epidemic. In the 1950s, epidemiologists found that smoking was a factor that almost all the people who developed lung cancer shared. This alone did not prove that smoking causes lung cancer. Epidemiology is not an experimental science where you can expose one group to a potentially harmful factor, such as cigarette smoke, and have a control group of people who do not smoke but are otherwise treated in exactly the same way. Experiments like this on humans are not ethical. However, epidemiological studies in other countries showed a strong association between smoking and lung cancer; this gave much evidence for the link (see Question 6 on page 65).

Experiments on dogs showed that smoking caused cancerous growths similar to human lung cancers; these did not occur in control groups. Laboratory rats and mice treated with substances isolated from cigarette smoke, such as benzpyrene, developed tumours. This showed that these substances are carcinogens. The results of these experiments show that there is a mechanism by which smoking can cause lung cancer and support the epidemiological evidence.

Coronary heart disease and stroke

Distribution of coronary heart disease

The prevalence of coronary heart disease differs across the world. The countries with the largest number of cases and highest mortality rates are in northern and eastern Europe. They are lowest in Mediterranean countries and in Japan. Death rates from CHD are falling in many places, but they are still very high in the UK and also in the old communist countries of eastern Europe, such as Latvia and the Russian Federation. However, the prevalence of CHD is rising in newly developed countries — it seems that CHD is associated with affluent lifestyles.

CHD has many causes, known as risk factors. Some of these are:
- poor diet — high intake of saturated fat and low intake of fresh fruit and vegetables
- smoking
- high blood cholesterol
- lack of exercise
- genetic factors

Figure 16 shows how nicotine and carbon monoxide contribute to the risk of developing CHD.

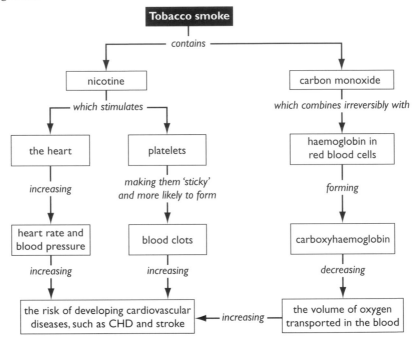

Figure 16 The effects of nicotine and carbon monoxide from tobacco smoke on the cardiovascular system

CHD and stroke often occur as a result of two events:
- a build-up of fatty material, known as plaque, inside the walls of arteries
- a blood clot

Atherosclerosis is the progressive build-up of plaque. It causes a blockage of the lumen of arteries and roughens the lining of arteries, so increasing the chances of blood clots forming. Build-up of plaque occurs because there is a lesion (or break) in the wall of an artery. Low-density lipoproteins enter the inner layer of arteries, and the cholesterol and fat they carry is oxidised, engulfed by macrophages that become foam cells and then all this fatty material stays there.

CHD occurs when there is an interruption in the supply of blood to the heart in the coronary arteries. See page 19 for a fuller explanation.

A stroke occurs when the blood supply in an artery to the brain is interrupted. This may happen because there is a blood clot or because the artery is weakened by plaque and bursts. Blood may leak into the brain tissue. This might be fatal. If not, then certain brain functions (such as speech and memory) may be impaired, either temporarily or permanently.

Prevention and cure

Cures for CHD are expensive. Drugs can be prescribed, but if the coronary arteries are beyond this then the fat can be removed by surgery using a procedure known as angioplasty. If this does not cure the condition, then bypass surgery may be carried out. This uses part of a vein from the leg to carry blood around a diseased coronary artery. Transplant surgery is also possible. This is more likely to be done for other reasons, such as for patients with cystic fibrosis, than for CHD. Transplants are often carried out on people requiring heart–lung transplants. The problems with transplants are the shortages of donors, finding a match and rejection of the organ by the immune system.

Screening the population for the risk factors listed above can help to identify those people most likely to develop CHD. Those who have an inherited disease that raises their blood cholesterol concentration are the highest priority. People with high blood pressure are also among those most at risk. Individuals can do something about some of the risk factors listed on page 31. They can reduce their intake of saturated fats, increase their intake of fresh fruit and vegetables, take more exercise, stop smoking and follow medical advice to lower blood pressure.

Preventing CHD is much cheaper than treating it. Providing drugs for large numbers of people to lower blood cholesterol and blood pressure is expensive. Operations such as coronary bypasses and heart transplants are very expensive and risky. In 1996, the UK government spent £1630 million on CHD: 32% of this was spent on drugs, 54% on hospital care. Only about 1% was spent on prevention.

Links This topic lends itself to data questions, such as Question 6 on page 65. You may be expected to calculate a mean, a percentage, a percentage change, mortality rates (perhaps as deaths per 100 000), incidence rates (cases per 100 000) or ratios.

In Module 2803/01, there is a section on the transport of carbon dioxide and oxygen. Both gases are transported by combining temporarily with haemoglobin. Carbon monoxide, however, combines permanently with haemoglobin and therefore reduces the amount of oxygen it can carry. Smokers show a 5–10% reduction in the quantity of oxygen transported in their blood compared with non-smokers.

In this section, you followed the epidemiological evidence for the link between smoking and disease. Questions on patterns of disease may be set on all areas in the module. Make sure that you can interpret graphs that show changes in incidence, prevalence or mortality from disease, such as lung cancer.

Infectious diseases

Cholera, malaria, TB and AIDS

Key concepts you must understand

Infectious diseases are caused by **pathogens** — organisms that invade the body and cause disease. Pathogens are transmitted from infected people to uninfected people. The four diseases in this section have all caused pandemics. Since the late 1980s, there has been a pandemic of HIV/AIDS; tuberculosis (TB) is now on the increase worldwide, partly as a result of widespread HIV infection. Malaria has been a major killer disease probably for the whole of human history and is still a huge medical problem in many African and Asian countries. There have been five major pandemics of cholera but it is now a much more restricted disease, although there is always a risk of it developing after natural catastrophes, such as earthquakes, or when many people are displaced and there is no sanitation (e.g. sewers).

Key facts you must know

Table 7 shows the organisms that cause these four diseases and how they are transmitted.

Disease	Causative organism	Type of organism	Method of transmission
Cholera	*Vibrio cholerae*	Bacterium — prokaryotic	Faecal–oral route — faeces from an infected person contaminate drinking water or food of an uninfected person
Malaria	*Plasmodium* species, e.g. *Plasmodium falciparum*	Protoctista — eukaryotic	*Anopheles* mosquito (vector) takes a blood meal from an infected person and then injects parasites in saliva when it takes a blood meal from an uninfected person
Tuberculosis	*Mycobacterium tuberculosis* (also *M. bovis* from cattle)	Bacterium — prokaryotic	Via droplets in the air — breathed out by an infected person and breathed in by an uninfected person
HIV/AIDS	Human immunodeficiency virus	RNA virus	From the bloodstream of an infected person to the bloodstream of an uninfected person during sexual intercourse; using shared needles; across the placenta; in breast milk; in donated blood or blood products

Table 7

The control of infectious diseases is carried out in several ways. Many diseases are controlled by vaccinations, but with these four diseases this is either not yet possible or of limited use. Control depends on taking various public health measures that often require considerable investment.

Control methods and problems with control

Cholera

Control method	Problems
Provide good sanitation to remove and treat human faeces so that bacteria are not transmitted from infected people	Providing good sewerage systems in many developing countries is economically not possible Sewage treatment is often disrupted by natural catastrophes, e.g. earthquakes and floods
Make sure that sewage does not contaminate drinking water by having separate sewerage and water systems	Many homes in developing countries do not have piped water Rivers may be used as both sewers and sources of drinking water
Make sure that people are supplied with clean drinking water which is treated to kill bacteria, e.g. by chlorination	Providing water treatment works and piping water to homes is not economically possible in many places
Fast treatment of infected people by oral rehydration therapy (salts and glucose in sterile water) and, in severe cases, with antibiotics	It is not always possible for medical staff to reach people in time, especially during emergencies There is no effective vaccine against cholera

Malaria

Control method	Problems
Stop mosquitoes breeding by destroying breeding areas (e.g. draining marshes) and spraying with insecticides	Some areas cannot be drained (e.g. nature reserves) *Anopheles* mosquitoes breed in very small bodies of water Mosquitoes are resistant to some insecticides, such as DDT (still used in developing countries)
Stop mosquitoes biting at night by using sleeping nets — this is most effective when nets are soaked in insecticide every 6 months	Difficult to provide nets and insecticides to remote populations Economically/politically difficult in many poor countries with civil unrest and/or poor infrastructure, e.g. difficult to reach remote districts
Use drugs to stop *Plasmodium* spreading through the human body Use drugs to treat people with malaria, so reducing the number of infected people who can pass on the disease to others via mosquitoes	*Plasmodium* has become resistant to many of these drugs There is no vaccine to control malaria

Tuberculosis (TB)

Control method	Problems
Quarantine people while they are in the infective stage and can transmit the disease to others	Problems with diagnosing the disease and finding facilities to quarantine people in developing countries
Use contact tracing to find people likely to have been infected	Only possible where there are health workers capable of doing this
Use antibiotics to treat infected people (course of treatment can be 6–12 months)	This is a long course of treatment; many do not finish it, thus increasing the risk of drug-resistant strains of TB emerging (see page 37)
Vaccinate people with BCG vaccine to give them active immunity (see page 42)	This is routine in the UK for children aged 13–14 but the BCG vaccine is not equally effective across the whole world
Test cattle for TB and destroy any that are infected. Pasteurise milk (TB can be transmitted from cattle to people)	TB testing is only possible where there are good veterinary services

HIV/AIDS

Control method	Problems
Educate the public about 'safer sex' — taking precautions during sex to limit chances of infection	People are often reluctant to change their sexual behaviour
Use condoms or femidoms during sexual intercourse	Danger that these may tear during sexual intercourse
Identify and treat people who are infected (and are referred to as HIV positive)	Only possible where good medical facilities exist. No cure for HIV/AIDS. No vaccine for HIV
Use contact tracing to find people likely to be infected	Only possible where there are health workers capable of doing this
Screen blood donors for HIV. Refuse donations from 'at risk' groups, such as sex workers. Treat blood donations and blood products to kill HIV	Routine in many countries but where these control measures do not happen there is a high risk of transmitting HIV

Antibiotics

Antibiotics are substances produced by microorganisms (or synthesised chemically) that are used to treat infectious diseases. They act on bacteria in one of three ways:

- They cause the bacteria to burst (lysis).
- They kill the bacteria without destroying them.
- They stop the bacteria reproducing.

They are not effective against viruses, although there are anti-viral drugs such as zidovudine, which is used for treatment of HIV/AIDS, and acyclovir, which is used to treat herpes.

Antibiotics are not equally effective against all bacteria. Doctors have to select the most effective antibiotic for each disease they treat. Some antibiotics have no effect at all on certain bacteria; others may be effective. It is best to find out before prescribing. A sample of bacteria can be taken from a patient and incubated with different antibiotics to find which is the most effective.

Antibiotic resistance

Bacteria become resistant to antibiotics because of random mutations in DNA. Normally, these mutant bacteria do not compete well with the non-mutant ('normal') forms. The normal forms are susceptible to being destroyed by antibiotics. When we use antibiotics the normal forms die leaving no competition for the mutant forms, which thrive as a result. Antibiotic resistance is a serious problem. Some bacterial diseases, such as TB, show resistance to many antibiotics (multi-drug resistance). As bacteria become resistant, this makes treating disease very difficult. We have been using antibiotics for over 50 years and there are now many resistant strains. To combat this, it is important that people should finish their course of antibiotics to make sure no pathogenic bacteria are left in their bodies. Antibiotics should not be overused for treating mild complaints and some should be kept as a last resort when all others have failed.

Note that bacterial resistance to antibiotics is *not* immunity. Immunity is a much more complicated process (see the next section). People do not become resistant to anti-biotics. Some people are allergic to certain antibiotics and they should not be prescribed these types.

Links The differences between the structures of prokaryotic and eukaryotic cells are covered in Module 2801. The organisms that cause TB and cholera are bacteria (prokaryotes). They have a simple cellular structure without a nucleus and with no membranous organelles, such as mitochondria or endoplasmic reticulum. *Plasmodium* is a eukaryote. It has a nucleus with a much greater genetic complexity than prokaryotes. This makes it a formidable enemy and explains why it is difficult to develop a vaccine against it. The surface antigens of *Plasmodium* can change and this makes vaccines ineffective, as we shall see in the next section. HIV infects T helper lymphocytes that control the immune response. This means that HIV infection leads to a gradual loss of the ability to respond to pathogens. AIDS is a collection of different diseases that attack people who do not have a fully functional immune system. Two of these 'opportunistic diseases' are a rare form of pneumonia and Kaposi's sarcoma, a rare cancer.

Immunity

The immune system

Key concepts you must understand

Our defence system consists of cells such as phagocytes and lymphocytes, and molecules such as antibodies. Phagocytic cells defend us by destroying invading organisms but they are not very effective on their own. We need a defence system that works specifically against the type of invading organism. Lymphocytes and antibodies provide this.

Key facts you must know

Phagocytes and lymphocytes originate in bone marrow.

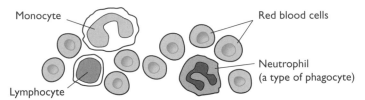

Figure 17 The different types of blood cell

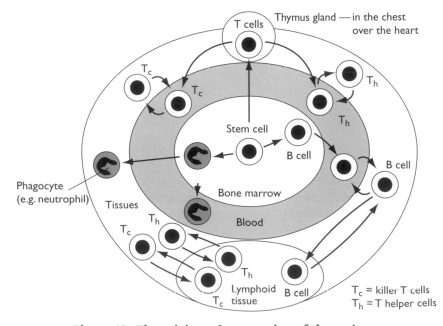

Figure 18 The origin and maturation of the major types
of cell involved in immunity

The origin, maturation and mode of action of phagocytes and lymphocytes

Phagocytes

We will consider two types of phagocyte — neutrophils and monocytes/macrophages.

Neutrophils circulate in the blood and spread into tissues during an infection. They are the 'rapid reaction force' of the immune system, responding quickly by rushing to an infected area and attempting to destroy any pathogens in the tissues (see Figure 19). They do not last long. After engulfing bacteria and destroying them, neutrophils die and sometimes accumulate to form pus.

Monocytes pass out of the bloodstream and enter tissues where they form **macrophages** (literally 'big eaters'). They are long-lived cells that have special roles to play in the immune response.

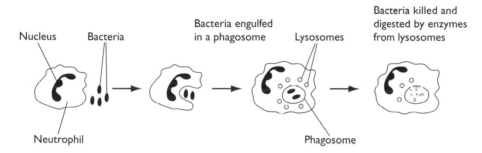

Figure 19 The stages involved in phagocytosis

Lymphocytes

B lymphocytes (**B cells** for short) originate and mature in bone marrow and then spread out through the body's lymphoid system. **T lymphocytes** (**T cells**) originate in bone marrow and migrate to the thymus where they mature. They then spread out through the lymphoid system.

As they mature, B and T lymphocytes gain their own unique cell surface receptors. These receptors are glycoproteins that are like antibody molecules. This gives them the ability to recognise specific antigens. There are small groups of specific B and T cells, each with their own receptors. Although there are many B and T cells in the body, there is only a small number of each type.

Pathogens and antigens

- A pathogen is a disease-causing organism (e.g. *Vibrio cholerae*, *Plasmodium*, *Mycobacterium* and HIV).
- An antigen is a molecule that can stimulate the formation of antibodies.
- Pathogens are covered in molecules (such as proteins and large carbohydrates) that have specific shapes and act as antigens.
- The immune system recognises any substance foreign to the body as antigenic.

The immune response

There are four stages in the immune response in which antibodies are produced (see Figure 20).

Stage 1 Antigen presentation

Macrophages in lymph nodes engulf pathogens by endocytosis and then 'cut them up'. These cells process antigens from the surface of the pathogen and put them into their own cell surface membranes.

Stage 2 Clonal selection

B cells and T cells with receptors complementary in shape to antigens lock onto the macrophage. Small groups of specific B and T cells are selected by the macrophage.

Stage 3 Clonal expansion

As there are very few cells with the capability of destroying the invading pathogen, these B and T cells divide by mitosis to form clones with many more cells. T helper cells release hormone-like chemicals called cytokines to stimulate B cells to divide.

Stage 4 Antibody production

The stimulated B cells form plasma cells, which secrete the appropriate antibody.

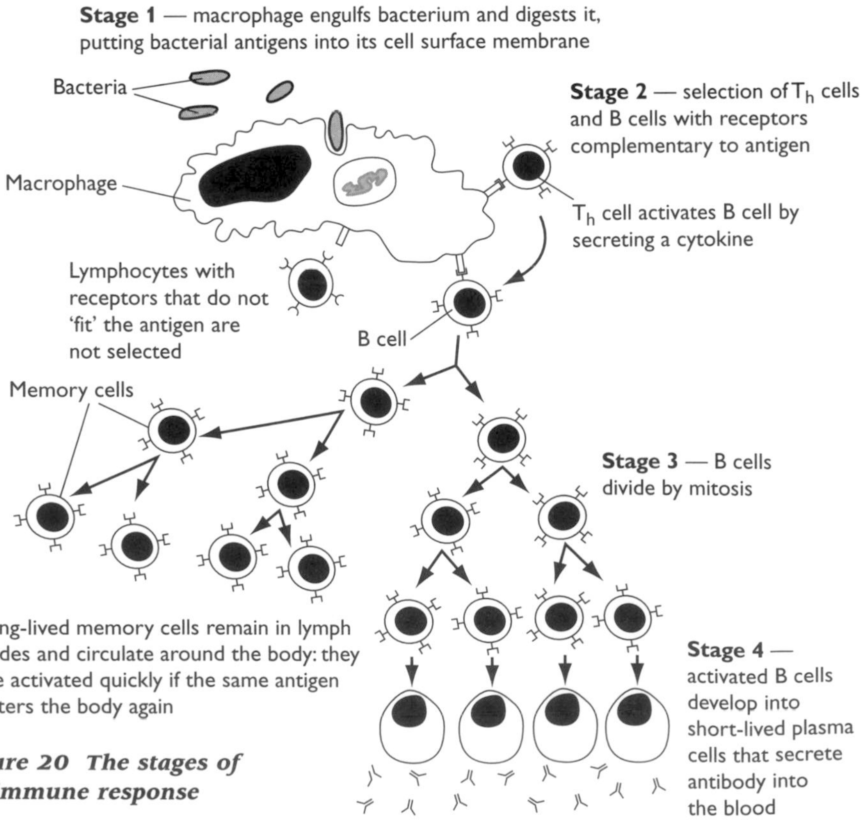

Figure 20 The stages of an immune response

Viruses invade our cells. They remain in the blood only for a short time. This means that antibodies against viruses do not work very well because they are only effective when viruses are in the blood. Antibodies are big molecules that cannot cross cell membranes to combine with viruses inside our cells. Some bacteria (e.g. the TB bacterium) invade cells too. During an immune response, killer T cells may be selected and stimulated to divide by mitosis so that they can attack host cells that have become infected by bacteria or viruses. Activated killer T cells latch onto the surface membrane of infected cells and kill the host cells by releasing toxic chemicals and enzymes.

Stages 1 to 4 take several days when an antigen enters the body for the first time — this is the **primary immune response**. This is why we are ill when we catch an infectious disease, such as measles. But after a while, antibodies and activated killer T cells are produced which help to remove the infectious agent and we recover. The whole process is much more efficient the next time because of memory cells.

Memory cells in long-term immunity

Plasma cells do not live long and soon the antibody molecules that they make begin to disappear from the blood. However, when an antigen enters the body for a second time, the response is much faster. This is because during **clonal expansion** (Stage 3), B cells form memory cells. These remain in the blood and lymph and respond much more quickly to a second infection by the same antigen because there are more of them than there were before the first infection.

A **secondary immune response** occurs much faster than the primary response and there are rarely any symptoms of the infection. Why is this? Remember that the clones of specific B and T cells that form during the maturation process have very few cells. Antigen presentation 'finds the right type of B cell and/or T cell' and then these cells divide. The memory cells are present in larger numbers than the original clone and they patrol the body 'on the look out' for the return of the same antigen.

Antibodies: very special proteins

It helps here to recall your knowledge of protein structure from Module 2801. Proteins are formed from polypeptides which are made of chains of amino acids. The simplest form of antibody molecule (known as immunoglobulin G, or IgG) is composed of four polypeptides. Each molecule has two antigen-binding sites that are identical — each binds with the same antigen (see Figure 21 on page 42). This binding is possible because the shape of the binding sites is complementary to that of the antigen. The antibody is specific to the antigen.

We make many antibody molecules with different binding sites to 'fit' around the different antigens that invade us. This is possible because amino acids can be arranged in different sequences to give a range of three-dimensional shapes. Because these binding sites vary, they are also called **variable regions**.

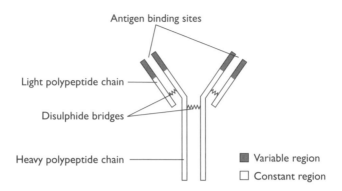

Figure 21 The structure of an antibody molecule (IgG)

Different types of immunity

So far we have considered what happens when an antigen enters the body. This is **active immunity**. It may happen naturally when you are infected or it may happen artificially when you are given a preparation, or **vaccine**, containing an antigen. Active immunity always involves an immune response (see above).

It is also possible to become immune by receiving antibodies from another person. This is **passive immunity**. Here the body gains an antibody from another source and has not come into contact with the antigen. No immune response occurs. Passive immunity may be gained naturally or artificially. The difference between active and passive immunity is shown in Figures 22 and 23.

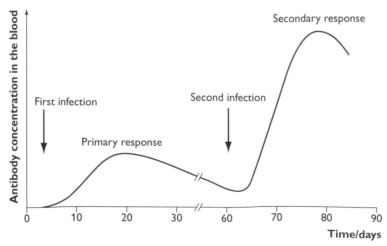

Figure 22 The change in antibody concentration during the primary and secondary response to the same antigen. This is what happens during active immunity.

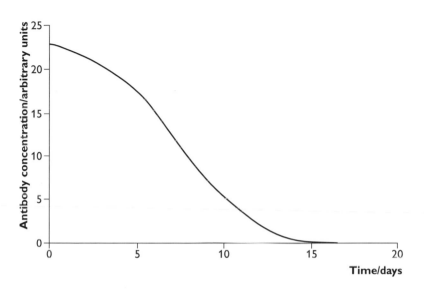

Figure 23 The change in antibody concentration in passive immunity. A person has been injected with antibodies. The concentration of antibodies decreases gradually because they are foreign to the body and are gradually removed. There are no activated lymphocytes (plasma cells) to secrete the antibody.

Allergies

Allergies, such as hay fever and asthma, are caused by the immune system over-reacting to harmless antigens known as **allergens**. Some allergens, such as pollen grains and the house dust mite and its faeces, are antigenic because they are covered by protein molecules. Some people become sensitised to these substances during a primary immune response. When the same substances are encountered again, there is an exaggerated secondary response, which can be serious.

The allergen for hay fever is most often grass or tree pollen. Hay fever is an unpleasant allergic reaction that leads to inflammation of the nose, eyes and throat. However, it is seasonal, only lasting as long as grass plants or trees are in flower and releasing pollen into the air.

Asthmatics may suffer attacks at any time. Inflammation occurs in the airways, such as the bronchi, which become filled with mucus and fluid leaking from the blood. Often, the muscles surrounding the airways contract as well. All this increases the resistance to air flow and asthmatics have great trouble in breathing.

When sensitisation occurs (Stages 1 and 2 in Figure 24 on page 44), T helper cells produce cytokines that stimulate B cells to form plasma cells (3) which secrete antibodies (4); they produce a type of antibody called IgE. These antibodies attach to receptors on mast cells. During an asthmatic attack (6) allergens combine with these antibodies (7) and this stimulates the mast cells to secrete histamine (8), which causes the inflammation (9).

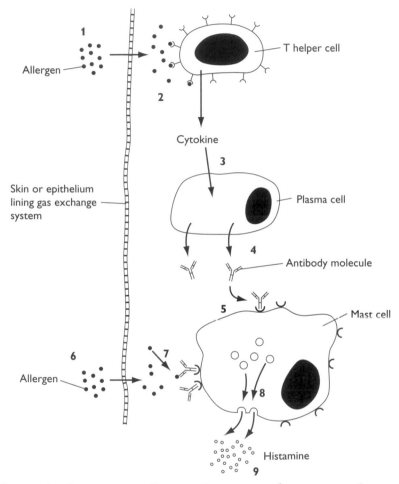

Figure 24 **The sequence of events that occurs when someone becomes sensitised to an allergen, which eventually results in an allergic response**

Vaccination controls disease

Vaccination is artificial active immunity. Vaccination may be used in two ways:
- **Herd immunity** — as many people as possible are vaccinated so that a pathogen cannot easily be transmitted from an infected person to an uninfected person because everyone, or nearly everyone, is immune. Vaccination programmes attempt to achieve nearly 100% coverage to achieve good herd immunity.

- **Ring immunity** — people living or working near someone infected (or their contacts) are vaccinated to prevent them catching the disease and then spreading it.

People who are vaccinated cannot harbour the pathogen and pass it on to others.

Why has smallpox been eradicated, but not measles, TB, malaria or cholera?

Smallpox was the first disease to be eradicated from the world. It is likely that polio will be the next. Smallpox was a terrible disease caused by a virus. It was suitable for eradication because:

- there was only one strain of the pathogen
- the virus did not infect animals
- it was easy to diagnose the disease
- any person who became infected with the virus developed symptoms of the disease — this meant that there were no carriers to act as a reservoir of viruses that could reinfect people

The vaccination programme, coordinated by the World Health Organization, was successful because:

- a 'live' vaccine was used, which meant that boosters were not necessary
- the vaccine was freeze-dried and so was suitable for use in the tropics
- only one vaccine was necessary and so was cheap to produce

Other diseases are more difficult to eradicate. Some of the reasons for this are:

- some pathogens exist in many strains which keep changing by mutation (e.g. influenza)
- the pathogens live in animals, for example malaria is transmitted by mosquitoes
- the pathogens invade the human gut where the immune system does not work very efficiently, for example cholera

It is difficult to develop vaccines against diseases that are caused by eukaryotic organisms, such as the malarial parasite *Plasmodium*, because they have many genes that code for cell surface antigens. Different strains of *Plasmodium* have different antigens. As *Plasmodium* passes through its different stages in liver and blood cells, it expresses different antigens. It also remains inside liver and red blood cells where antibodies have no effect.

It is not easy to organise vaccination programmes for measles, which primarily affects young children. Often, in less economically developed countries, it is impossible to vaccinate infants soon enough after birth to give them protection when they are vulnerable to infection. Measles is an infectious disease that spreads quickly, especially in overcrowded cities.

Questions
&
Answers

This section is not exactly like the unit test. Each question is based mainly on one of the sections in the module. In the unit test, you will find that parts of each question may require information from two or more sections of the module. For example, Question 7 (on page 68) is mainly about infectious diseases, but part (e) is set on the immunity section. You should be prepared for this when you take the unit test.

As you read through this section, you will find that Candidate A gains full marks for all the questions. This is so you can see what high-grade answers look like. Remember that the minimum for a grade A is about 80% of the maximum mark for the paper (48 out of 60 for the unit test). Candidate B makes a lot of mistakes — these are ones that examiners encounter quite frequently. I will tell you how many marks Candidate B gets for each question. If the overall mark for the paper is about 40% of the total (24 marks in the unit test), then this candidate will just fail to pass.

Examiner's comments

Candidates' answers are followed by examiner's comments. These are preceded by the icon *e* and indicate where credit is due. In the weaker answers they also point out areas for improvement, specific problems and common errors, such as lack of clarity, weak or non-existent development, irrelevance, misinterpretation of the question and mistaken meanings of terms.

Introduction to health and disease

Diseases or illnesses are classified into categories. Some diseases may be classified into more than one category.

(a) Complete the table below by indicating with a tick (✓) the category or categories in which each of the diseases is classified. (4 marks)

Disease	Physical	Infectious	Degenerative	Deficiency
Night blindness				
Cholera				
Coronary heart disease				
Measles				

(b) Explain why tuberculosis (TB) may be described as a *social disease*. (1 mark)

(c) TB is endemic in populations across the whole world. Define the term *endemic*. (1 mark)

Table 1 shows information published by the World Health Organization about causes of death in Europe and Africa in 1998.

Cause of death	Africa			Europe		
	Rank order	Number of deaths	% of total	Rank order	Number of deaths	% of total
Acute lower respiratory infections, e.g. pneumonia	3	787 200	8.2	4	334 800	3.6
Chronic bronchitis and emphysema	14	105 600	1.1	5	251 100	2.7
Coronary heart disease	9	278 400	2.9	1	2 371 500	25.5
Diarrhoeal diseases, e.g. cholera	4	729 600	7.6	22	65 100	0.7
HIV/AIDS	1	1 824 000	19.0	42	18 600	0.2
Lung cancer	38	28 800	0.3	3	390 600	4.2
Malaria	2	960 000	10.0	–	–	–
Stroke	7	451 200	4.7	2	1 274 100	13.7
Tuberculosis	11	211 200	2.2	23	55 800	0.6
Other causes		4 224 000	44.0		4 538 400	48.8
Totals		9 600 000	100		9 300 000	100

Table 1

The populations of Europe and Africa were estimated as 870 million and 601 million respectively in 1998. The mortality rate in Europe in 1998 was 1069 deaths per 100 000 of the population.

(d) Using the information provided and the data in Table 1:
  (i) Calculate the mortality rate in Africa as number of deaths per **100 000** of the population. Show your working and express your answer to the nearest whole number. (2 marks)
  (ii) State the advantage of expressing the causes of death as percentages of the total deaths for each continent. (2 marks)
  (iii) Describe the differences between the leading causes of death in Europe and Africa. (3 marks)
  (iv) Suggest how the World Health Organization may use the statistics shown in Table 1. (2 marks)

Total: 15 marks

■ ■ ■

Candidates' answers to Question 1

Candidate A

(a)

Disease	Physical	Infectious	Degenerative	Deficiency
Night blindness	✓			✓
Cholera	✓	✓		
Coronary heart disease	✓		✓	
Measles	✓	✓		

Candidate B

(a)

Disease	Physical	Infectious	Degenerative	Deficiency
Night blindness	✓			✗
Cholera		✓		
Coronary heart disease			✓	
Measles		✓		

e Candidate A has answered the question correctly. Candidate B has not realised that all the diseases given are physical diseases and also thinks that it is only necessary to put one tick in each row. The answer for night blindness could be correct, but a crossed tick (✗) is always taken to be a cross by the examiner. Sometimes the question asks for crosses *and* ticks for these tables. If you put a cross and want to change it into a tick, strike out the cross completely and start again — don't try to convert a cross to a tick or a tick to a cross. Candidate B gains no marks here.

Candidate A

(b) Tuberculosis is transmitted when people live and sleep (especially) in overcrowded places. Their living conditions make this a social disease.

Candidate B

(b) TB is caught by people who live in small, cramped houses.

> *e* Candidate A has identified an appropriate reason for categorising TB as a social
> disease. Candidate B has made a common mistake about the conditions that favour
> the transmission of TB. It is not the size of people's houses that matters — it is
> whether they live and sleep close together, so that bacteria breathed out by
> infected people can easily be breathed in by uninfected people. Transmission of TB
> is more likely when people share the same sleeping area, especially in rooms that
> are poorly ventilated.

Candidate A

(c) Endemic means that TB is always present in a population.

Candidate B

(c) It affects large numbers of people all over the world.

> *e* Candidate A has the right answer. Candidate B is confusing *endemic* with *pandemic*,
> possibly because the question says 'across the whole world'.

Candidate A

(d) (i) $\dfrac{9\,600\,000}{601\,000\,000} \times 100\,000 = 1597$

Candidate B

(d) (i) $\dfrac{9\,600\,000}{601\,000\,000} \times 100\,000 = 1597.338$

> *e* Candidate B has calculated the number of deaths correctly and gains 1 mark for
> showing the working, but has not answered the question. The answer should be
> rounded down to 1597.

Candidate A

(d) (ii) So a valid comparison can be made, because the populations are different
in Africa and Europe. There are 270 million more people in Europe than in Africa.

Candidate B

(d) (ii) This is so that you can make a fair comparison between the two countries.

> *e* Both candidates have made the 'valid comparison' point, which is worth 1 mark.
> Candidate A has used the figures, as instructed at the beginning of the question, for
> the second mark. *Any* appropriate use of the figures would gain a mark. Another
> way to express the figures in Table 1 would be to calculate them as death rates *per
> 100 000*.

Candidate A

(d) (iii) The leading causes of death in Europe are diseases of old age, such as coronary
heart disease and lung cancer. These are degenerative diseases.

The leading causes of death in Africa are infectious diseases, such as HIV/AIDS and malaria. Nearly 40% of deaths in Africa were caused by infectious diseases, but the same diseases only caused about 5% of deaths in Europe.

Candidate B

(d) (iii) The leading cause of death in Africa was HIV/AIDS (19%). In Europe it was coronary heart disease (25.5%).

Candidate A has grouped the leading causes of death and has noticed that in Africa, which has mainly middle- and low-income countries, these are infectious diseases. European countries generally have good control measures for infectious diseases and their populations have a good life expectancy. The leading causes of death are long-term degenerative diseases, such as coronary heart disease. Candidate B is awarded 1 mark for using the figures.

Candidate A

(d) (iv) Because the WHO knows that some diseases, like AIDS, are very important in Africa, it can help governments develop ways of combating the spread of the disease. They could do this by sending doctors or scientists to countries in Africa. It can also use the figures to publicise the problem.

Candidate B

(d) (iv) These figures help to show people which are the most important diseases in different parts of the world.

Candidate A has given a good suggestion and has used some information from the table. Candidate B has written a rather vague answer which does not gain any marks.

Candidate B scores 3 marks out of 15 for this question.

Question 2

Diet

(a) Identify the component or components of a balanced diet best described by each of the following:

   (i) a mineral element required for the synthesis of haem
   (ii) a compound that prevents the deficiency disease xerophthalmia
   (iii) a compound required for the synthesis of phospholipids in cell membranes
   (iv) a material that reduces the likelihood of constipation
   (v) nitrogen-containing compounds that cannot be synthesised by the body   (5 marks)

The body mass index (**BMI**) is calculated using the following formula:

$$\text{BMI} = \frac{\text{body mass in kg}}{(\text{height in metres})^2}$$

Table 1 shows the categories for BMI.

BMI	Category
Below 20	Underweight
20–25	Acceptable
25–30	Overweight
30–40	Obese
Over 40	Very obese

Table 1

(b) Complete the table below by:
   (i) calculating the BMI for person C
   (ii) using Table 1 to identify the appropriate category for this person   (2 marks)

Person	Height/m	Mass/kg	BMI	Category
A	1.60	60	23	Acceptable
B	1.65	48	18	Underweight
C	1.50	74		

(c) Suggest an advantage for health of maintaining a BMI within the acceptable range.   (2 marks)

In the human body, vitamin **D** is converted by enzymes into 'active' vitamin **D**, which acts as a hormone that targets the gut and skeleton.

(d) Describe the effects of 'active' vitamin **D** on the gut and skeleton.   (2 marks)

The Reference Nutrient Intake (**RNI**) is one of the dietary reference values. Table 2 shows the RNIs for vitamin D.

2

question

Age	RNI/µg day^{-1}
0–6 months	8.5
7 months–3 years	7.0
4–64 years	0
65 years and over	10.0
Pregnant women	10.0
Breast-feeding women	10.0

Table 2

(e) **Explain why the RNI for vitamin D is zero for those aged between 4 and 64.** (2 marks)

(f) **Explain why it is important for women who are pregnant or breast feeding to ensure that their diet contains vitamin D.** (3 marks)

Total: 16 marks

■ ■ ■

Candidates' answers to Question 2

Candidate A

(a) (i) iron
   (ii) vitamin A
   (iii) linoleic acid
   (iv) fibre
   (v) essential amino acids

Candidate B

(a) (i) iron
   (ii) vitamin D
   (iii) essential fatty acids
   (iv) cellulose
   (v) amino acids

   ✍ Candidate B's answers to (i), (iii) and (iv) are correct, for 3 marks. In (ii), the candidate has confused vitamin D with vitamin A; in (v) the word 'essential' must be included.

Candidate A

(b) (i) 33
   (ii) obese

Candidate B

(b) (i) 49
   (ii) very obese

e When calculating the BMI, it is necessary to take the square of the height. Candidate B has forgotten to do this. The examiner would carry forward an error here and award 1 mark for choosing the appropriate category for the answer that has been calculated. You do not need to remember the formula for BMI; it will be provided in the test.

Candidate A

(c) There are many health risks associated with obesity. Two of these are an increased risk of developing coronary heart disease and arthritis.

Candidate B

(c) The acceptable body mass index means that they are not putting on fat or becoming too thin.

e Candidate B has not identified any of the risks to health associated with 'putting on fat'. The health risks associated with anorexia would also be acceptable here.

Candidate A

(d) It stimulates the bones to take calcium from the blood and store it. It stimulates the gut to absorb calcium.

Candidate B

(d) Vitamin D causes bones to use calcium to become harder.

e Candidate A gives correct information about *both* the gut and the bones. Candidate B only answers half the question, but gives enough information to gain 1 mark.

Candidate A

(e) This is because the amount of vitamin D which we need is synthesised by the body when the skin is exposed to ultraviolet light.

Candidate B

(e) This is because we absorb vitamin D from the sun.

e Candidate A gives a correct answer — vitamin D is synthesised from other compounds in the skin when exposed to ultraviolet light. We make enough vitamin D during the summer months to last us the rest of the year, since it is stored in muscle tissue. Candidate B makes a common mistake in thinking that vitamin D is *in* sunlight and is absorbed when we expose our skin. This is not correct.

Candidate A

(f) Young children need vitamin D to prevent rickets. Obviously, unborn babies are not exposed to sunlight to make what they need, so it has to be provided by the mother. This makes sure the child does not suffer from a deficiency.

Candidate B

(f) This is to make sure the baby gets enough vitamin D. If it doesn't it may suffer from a deficiency and suffer from night blindness and maybe total blindness. A deficiency also causes a dry cornea in the eye.

e Candidate B has confused vitamin A with vitamin D again, so does not receive any marks. It is a deficiency of vitamin A that causes night blindness, total blindness and a dry cornea. There would be a mark available in this question for describing the effects of rickets, such as softening of the bones and bowing of the leg bones under the weight of the rest of the body.

e **Candidate B scores 5 marks out of 16 for this question.**

The gaseous exchange system

Figure 1 is a drawing of part of the wall of the trachea, as seen with the light microscope.

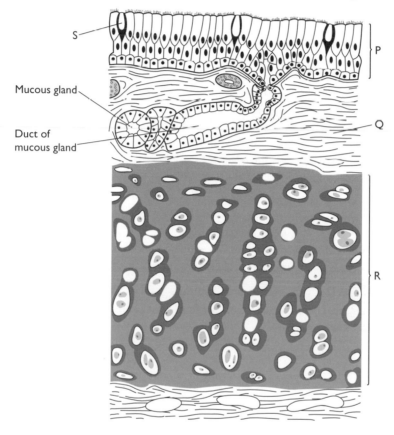

Figure 1

(a) **Name:**
- (i) the tissues labelled **P** and **R** (2 marks)
- (ii) the fibres labelled **Q** (1 mark)
- (iii) the cell labelled **S** (1 mark)

(b) Describe the role of the mucous glands in the trachea. (3 marks)

Total: 7 marks

■ ■ ■

Candidates' answers to Question 3

Candidate A

(a) (i) **P**: ciliated epithelium
   R: cartilage

(ii) Q: elastic fibres

(iii) S: goblet cell

Candidate B

(a) (i) P: epithelium

R: muscle

(ii) Q: elastin

(iii) S: goblet cell

e Candidate A has identified all the parts correctly. Candidate B gains 3 marks for epithelium (although 'ciliated' should really appear in the answer as well), goblet cell and elastin (which is an acceptable alternative to elastic fibres). Cartilage (**R**) is quite different in appearance from muscle, which is not in the section shown in Figure 1. There is smooth muscle at the back of the trachea between the two 'ends' of the C-shaped rings of cartilage. You might see this if looking at sections of trachea under a microscope.

Candidate A

(b) These glands secrete mucus that travels up the duct onto the surface of the trachea. It is sticky, so dust particles and bacteria stick to it. The cilia move the mucus up the trachea towards the throat. This helps to protect the alveoli from damage by dust and by pathogens.

Candidate B

(b) Mucus is sticky and forms a carpet over the cilia in the trachea. Things such as bacteria and spores stick to it.

e Candidate A states the function of the mucous glands and makes use of information from the figure. The word 'role' in the question means more than just 'what the glands do'. Candidate A has explained that the mucus produced by the gland protects the alveoli; you should write about the wider context when you see the word 'role'. The learning outcomes for this section do not mention the mucous glands, but you should be able to apply your knowledge of goblet cells to explain the role of the mucous glands. Candidate B gains 2 marks here.

e **Candidate B is awarded 5 marks out of 7 for this question.**

Question 4

Exercise (1)

A student carried out an investigation to find the effect of a period of strenuous exercise on the heart rate of a college athlete. The athlete's heart rate was recorded before, during and after the exercise. Immediately before the exercise, the athlete went through a period of 'warming up'. The results are shown in Figure 1.

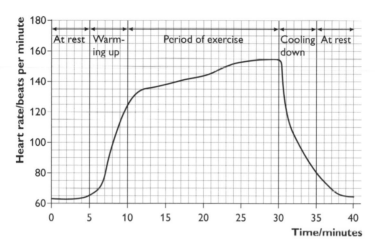

Figure 1

(a) Use the data in Figure 1 to answer the following questions:
  (i)   State the maximum heart rate achieved during the period of exercise. (1 mark)
  (ii) Suggest *one* advantage of 'warming up' before starting strenuous exercise. (2 marks)
  (iii) The volume of blood expelled by the athlete's heart during exercise was estimated as 130 cm³ per beat. Calculate the volume of blood pumped out by the heart in dm³ per minute at the end of the period of exercise. Show your working and express your answer to the nearest whole number. (2 marks)
  (iv) Calculate the percentage decrease in the heart rate during the 'cool down' period at the end of the exercise. Show your working and express your answer to the nearest whole number. (2 marks)
(b) In this question, 1 mark is available for the quality of written communication. Explain why the heart rate does not return immediately to the resting value after the end of a period of strenuous exercise. You will gain credit for using information from Figure 1. (8 marks)

Total: 15 marks

question 4

Candidates' answers to Question 4

Candidate A

(a) (i) 155 beats per minute

(ii) The heart rate starts to increase from 65 to 125 beats per minute, so supplying oxygen to the muscles in readiness for exercise.

(iii) $155 \times 130 = 20150 \, cm^3 = 20.15 \, dm^3$ per minute

$$= 20 \, dm^3 \text{ per minute}$$

(iv) $155 - 80 = 75$

$$\frac{75}{155} \times 100 = 48.39 = 48\% \text{ decrease}$$

Candidate B

(a) (i) 155 bpm

(ii) The athlete stretches the muscles before starting.

(iii) $155 \times 130 = 20150 \, cm^3$ per minute

(iv) $\dfrac{80}{155} \times 100 = 51.61\%$

Both candidates gain a mark for part (i); Candidate B has used an abbreviation for the unit (beats per minute) which is fine and far better than not giving any units at all. Often the units are given in the question or on an answer line, but it is good practice always to write the units after any numbers you take from a graph like this. Candidate A gains 2 marks in (ii) for making a reference to the figure and giving one sensible explanation. Candidate B has not used the figure or explained how 'stretching the muscle' is beneficial. In (iii), both candidates gain a mark for the working, but only Candidate A gets full marks because Candidate B has forgotten to divide by 1000 to give the answer in dm^3 rather than cm^3. Candidate A has calculated the percentage decrease in (iv) correctly, but Candidate B has calculated the heart rate at the end of the 'cooling down' period (80 bpm) as a percentage of the highest heart rate (155 bpm). A percentage change is calculated as:

$$\frac{\text{difference}}{\text{original}} \times 100 \quad not \quad \frac{\text{final}}{\text{original}} \times 100$$

Candidate A

(b) During exercise (especially at the start), the muscles do not receive enough oxygen and so some anaerobic respiration occurs. This is because there is a high demand made on the body for an instant supply of energy for muscle contraction. It takes some time to reach the maximum heart rate. In fact it takes about 15 minutes. During this time, the athlete is building up an oxygen deficit because not enough oxygen is getting to the muscles. Anaerobic respiration in muscles produces lactate and this diffuses out into the blood. It is still in the blood at the end of exercise and is taken up by the liver and respired to carbon dioxide and water. Some is also converted to glucose. This process needs oxygen, which explains why the heart rate is still high. This is known as the oxygen debt. Stores of oxygen (in myoglobin) in muscles have been used up and need to be replaced. During 'cool down' the heart beats quite fast, but does not pump out blood as quickly as the $19\,dm^3$ per minute it was during exercise. The heart helps to use up some of the lactate. Heart muscle respires lactate.

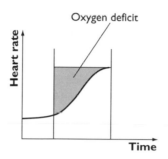

Candidate B

(b) During exercise, the body is using energy faster than it can produce oxygen. The body goes from respiring aerobically to breathing anaerobically. It produces a lot of lactic acid as the glucose is used up. During the 'oxygen dept' the heart beat slows down.

✏ This is the extended answer question. Candidate A writes a full answer, using some figures both from the graph and answers to part (a). There would be 2 marks available for quoting figures from the graph. The candidate also explains that anaerobic respiration occurs, leading to an oxygen deficit. This is identified with a sketch (which is an excellent idea) and the oxygen debt is explained in straight-forward terms to gain full marks. The candidate gains a quality of written communication mark for punctuation, grammar and spelling.

Candidate B has made a typical mistake when writing about exercise — referring to the 'body' rather than to muscles. The relationship between the energy demand of the muscles, the oxygen required for aerobic respiration and the two types of respiration is confused. The candidate has mentioned lactic acid but not explained why it is produced. No figures from the graph have been used. It is unlikely that this answer will gain any marks. The quality mark is not awarded because the answer is poorly organised and expressed. Debt is spelt 'dept', which is a common mistake.

✏ **Candidate B gains 2 marks out of 15 for this question.**

Question 5

Exercise (2)

A student designed an investigation to find out how much exercise was necessary to improve the aerobic fitness of a group of 17-year-olds. The student planned the investigation as follows:

Select 20 people who do not take exercise on a regular basis.

(1) Organise the group into pairs, matching them for gender, age, body mass and height.
(2) Select one member from each pair to carry out the training programme.
(3) The training involves swimming several lengths of a swimming pool at a fixed speed so that the pulse rate reaches approximately 70% of the age-predicted maximum (calculated by subtracting the person's age from 220).
(4) Training should occur for 20 minutes on three occasions every week.
(5) Measure the resting pulse rate of the whole group (those carrying out the training and those who are not) at regular intervals.

  (a) In this investigation:
    (i) explain why the resting pulse rate is recorded throughout   (2 marks)
    (ii) state *one* advantage of measuring resting pulse rate   (1 mark)

  (b) Explain why:
    (i) the student selected people who did not take exercise on a regular basis
    (ii) one of each pair did *not* follow the training programme
    (iii) the subjects were matched for gender, body mass, age and height
    (iv) the subjects exercised at approximately 70% of their maximum pulse rate   (4 marks)

  (c) Suggest how the student could analyse the data collected from this investigation to find out if there was a significant improvement in aerobic fitness.   (2 marks)

  (d) Explain why swimming for 20 minutes is better than weightlifting for improving aerobic fitness.   (2 marks)

  (e) State *one* long-term consequence of exercise on muscle.   (1 mark)

Total: 12 marks

■ ■ ■

Candidates' answers to Question 5

Candidate A
(a) (i) A low resting pulse means that someone has good aerobic fitness.
   (ii) It does not need any complicated apparatus.

Candidate B
(a) (i) It is one way of measuring fitness.
   (ii) You can take it at any time of the day. It is easy to take.

   ✏ In (i), Candidate B has left out the key word here which is 'aerobic'. Part (ii) is not meant to be a trick question. It is easy to take the resting pulse and it can be taken at any time of the day, although in such an investigation it should be taken at the same time of day and is best taken first thing in the morning. Candidate B gains 1 mark here.

Candidate A

(b) (i) So he/she could see a significant improvement in fitness.
  (ii) That person was the control.
  (iii) To make valid comparisons.
  (iv) This is recommended as being good for improving aerobic fitness.

Candidate B

(b) (i) Someone who is not very fit should get fitter during the training.
  (ii) To compare the results against.
  (iii) So that the investigation was a 'fair test'.
  (iv) Exercising less than this might not have any effect on fitness.

  e Candidate B scores 3 marks. At AS and A2 it is expected that candidates explain the term 'fair test' if they use it. 'To make valid comparisons', as given by Candidate A, is a much better answer.

Candidate A

(c) He could plot a graph to see how the resting pulse changes during the training programme. The resting pulse of the students who did the exercise should decrease and show an improvement in fitness. A statistical test could be used to see if the decrease is significant.

Candidate B

(c) Calculate the percentage decrease in the results from the beginning to the end of the training. Then compare the person who did the training with the person who didn't.

  e Both these answers would gain the 2 marks. There are three things to note:
  - At AS it is not necessary for you to use statistical tests. Candidate A may have done statistics at GCSE and knows that you can find out if results are significantly different by using such a test.
  - Candidate B has looked at the difference between the people who exercised and the control group. This is a good way of analysing the results. Calculating percentage change (decrease in resting pulse divided by resting pulse at the start of the investigation × 100) is a good way of quantifying the effect without doing a statistical test.
  - The learning outcome states that you should know how to carry out an investigation to find how much exercise is necessary for significant improvement in fitness. This is one way in which this investigation could be done.

Candidate A

(d) Swimming is aerobic exercise in which the heart and lungs work harder to supply oxygen to the muscles. Weightlifting would be good for muscle building but the muscles use anaerobic respiration, not aerobic.

Candidate B

(d) Swimming involves aerobic respiration.

5

> *e* When asked to compare two things ('why swimming is better than weightlifting') it is always a good idea to write something about both. Candidate A does this but Candidate B only writes about swimming. Candidate A gets 2 marks for 'aerobic exercise' and for referring to 'heart and lungs'. The comment on weightlifting would have scored too. Candidate B gains no credit here.

Candidate A

(e) More mitochondria are formed in the muscle cells.

Candidate B

(e) They get more blood capillaries.

> *e* Both answers are correct. Note that the question says 'muscle'. Answers on heart, lungs or any other part of the body would be incorrect. Both candidates have read the question carefully.

> *e* **Candidate B is awarded 7 marks out of 12 for this question.**

Smoking and disease

(a) State *one* effect of each of the following constituents of cigarette smoke on the cardiovascular system
- nicotine
- carbon monoxide   (2 marks)

(b) Complete the following passage about lung cancer by using the most appropriate word (or words).

Cigarette smoke contains substances known as .... which stimulate changes in DNA. These changes are known as .... and they increase the chances that cells in the lining of the bronchus will start to divide uncontrollably by .... A cell that starts to divide in this way may, after many years, form a group of cells known as a .... These cells may block the airways or blood vessels and may break off and spread to other parts of the body. One of the symptoms of lung cancer is

....   (5 marks)

A long-term study of the effects of smoking on health was undertaken in the **USA**. A large group of people was divided into two groups. One group consisted of smokers (**A**), the control group consisted of non-smokers (**B**). When these people died their cause of death was recorded. Table 1 shows the results of the study.

Cause of death	Deaths among smokers (A)	Deaths among non-smokers (B)	Excess of deaths (A – B)	Percentage of excess (A – B/total of excess deaths)	Relative death rate (A/B)
CHD	3361	1973	1388	52.1	1.70
Stroke	556	428	128	4.8	1.30
Lung cancer	397	37	360	13.5	10.73
Cancer of mouth and oesophagus	91	18	73	....	....
Other causes	2911	2195	716	26.9	1.33
Total deaths (all causes)	**7316**	**4651**	**2665**	**100.0**	**1.57**

Table 1

For each disease in Table 1:
- the number of excess deaths is calculated as the difference between the number of deaths among the smokers and the number among the non-smokers
- the contribution of each disease to the total of excess deaths is given as the percentage of the excess

- the relative death rate is calculated as the number of deaths in the smoker group divided by the number among the non-smokers. This is a measure of the *risk* of smoking leading to each of the diseases in the table.

(c) Suggest *two* precautions that should be taken when choosing the non-smokers for the control group in a study of this type. (2 marks)

(d) Complete the table by calculating for cancer of the mouth and oesophagus:
   (i) the percentage of excess
   (ii) the relative death rate (2 marks)

(e) A student who analysed these results concluded that 'smoking causes more deaths from cardiovascular disease than from lung cancer'. Explain whether the data in Table 1 support this statement or not. You will gain credit if you use the data from the table in your answer. (4 marks)

Total: 15 marks

■ ■ ■

Candidates' answers to Question 6

Candidate A

(a) Nicotine increases heart rate; carbon monoxide combines irreversibly with haemo-globin.

Candidate B

(a) Nicotine makes platelets in the blood more sticky; carbon monoxide combines with oxygen, so less is carried in the blood.

> 𝑒 The effect of carbon monoxide is to lower the volume of oxygen carried by the blood. Candidate A is correct in that it does this by combining with haemoglobin. Candidate B makes a common mistake, and scores no mark for this part of the answer, but gains 1 mark for making a correct statement about nicotine.

Candidate A

(b) carcinogens; mutations; mitosis; tumour; pain in the chest, blood in sputum

Candidate B

(b) carcogens; mutations; mitosis; tumor; coughing up blood.

> 𝑒 Candidate B has not spelt 'carcinogens' correctly and does not gain a mark. 'Tumor' is the American spelling, so it is acceptable. Candidate B scores 4 marks. It is important to spell words correctly; American spellings of words, such as hemoglobin, sulfur and, in this case tumor, are acceptable. Candidate A gives two symptoms of lung cancer, although the question asks for one. There is no penalty here, as both are correct.

Candidate A

(c) None of them should have smoked in the past or lived with a smoker (passive smoking).

Candidate B

(c) They should all be the same age, gender and ethnic group.

> *e* Candidate A makes two interesting points. The risk of developing smoking-related diseases is higher for past smokers and for passive smokers than it is for non-smokers, so it is important that these groups are excluded from the control group. Candidate B makes three points, not two, but they are all correct, for 2 marks. Examiners do not pick correct answers from a list, so make sure you give the number required.

Candidate A

(d) (i) 2.7%   (ii) 5.06

Candidate B

(d) (i) 2.73%   (ii) 0.20

> *e* Candidate B has given the answer in (i) to 2 decimal places, whereas the others in the table are given to 1. Since the question does not specify how to express the answer, it is likely that a mark would be awarded here. It is usually best (if you are not told otherwise) to give the same number of decimal places as the other figures in the table in questions of this type. In (ii), Candidate B has divided column B by column A instead of the other way around. This answer (0.20) suggests that smoking *reduces* the risk of developing cancer of the mouth and oesophagus.

Candidate A

(e) Yes. I would agree. The data show that smoking increases the risk of getting lung cancer by 10 times. Among the people studied, 360 more died from lung cancer than might have been expected to die from that disease. For CHD the risk is 1.70 (stroke = 1.30) which means there is a much lower risk, but 1516 more people died of CVD (CHD + stroke) than might have been expected if smoking had no effect. This is 56.9% of the 'excess' deaths.

Candidate B

(e) More people died of coronary heart disease than any other. This shows that it is the biggest cause of death. Only 397 smokers died of lung cancer compared with 3361 from CHD.

> *e* Candidate A has really 'got into' the data in the table and understands the concept of risk very well. The answer shows that the candidate knows that stroke and CHD are both cardiovascular diseases (CVDs). Candidate A has also said that the statement is correct. When answering this type of question be prepared to agree or disagree with the statement, and to provide evidence to support your case. Questions may be set in which there is evidence that supports the statement and also some that does not. In such cases, there will be marks for both agreeing and disagreeing with the statement, so long as you give some evidence in support of your answer. Candidate B gains 1 mark here for using the figures to make a comparison.

> *e* **Candidate B scores 9 marks out of 15 for this question.**

Question 7

Infectious diseases

(a) **Name the organism that causes malaria.** (1 mark)

(b) **Describe how malaria is transmitted.** (3 marks)

'Roll Back Malaria' is the World Health Organization's programme for restricting the spread of malaria. The disease is particularly important in Africa, where trials of vaccines are currently being conducted. The genome of *Plasmodium* has been sequenced and this may make it easier to develop vaccines and drugs for controlling malaria. Figure 1 shows the changes in mortality from malaria during the twentieth century in Africa and in the rest of the world.

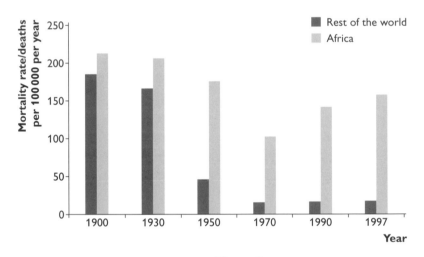

Figure 1

(c) **Describe the trends in the pattern of mortality from malaria in Africa and the rest of the world in the twentieth century. Credit will be given if you use data from Figure 1 in your answer.** (4 marks)

(d) **Explain the pattern that you have described in part (c).** (4 marks)

(e) **Explain the *biological* reasons that have made it difficult to develop a vaccine against malaria.** (3 marks)

Total: 15 marks

■ ■ ■

Candidates' answers to Question 7

Candidate A
(a) *Plasmodium*

Candidate B
(a) A virus

🖉 Many people think that it is a virus that causes malaria and this is incorrect. *Plasmodium* is the scientific name for the organism that causes malaria and it is this name that you should give. *Plasmodium* is a protoctistan.

Candidate A

(b) A female *Anopheles* mosquito feeds on someone who is infected with malaria. The malarial parasite reproduces inside the mosquito and enters its salivary glands. When the mosquito feeds again, it injects the parasite into the blood of someone who is not infected.

Candidate B

(b) Mosquitoes transmit the disease. They pass it on when they bite people.

🖉 Candidate A has given a very full answer using the terms *infected* and *uninfected* when describing transmission. You should do this when describing transmission of any of the four infectious diseases in this section of the module. Candidate B has mentioned mosquitoes, so gains a mark. The answer does not explain how the disease is transmitted to someone previously uninfected.

Candidate A

(c) Deaths from malaria have decreased greatly in the rest of the world from about 195 per 100 000 in 1900 to just under 20 in 1997. The mortality rate has always been higher in Africa, decreasing from over 220 to about 110 per 100 000 in 1970; then it increased again to about 165 in 1997.

Candidate B

(c) The death rate in Africa was 225 000 in 1900. In 1997 it was 160 000. During the twentieth century, it went down and then went up. DDT was used to control mosquitoes in Africa and this is why there were fewer deaths in the middle part of the century.

🖉 Candidate A has given a good, concise answer and made excellent use of the data. It is not necessary to quote the units for every figure when they are the same throughout the answer, but they need to be made clear at the beginning. Candidate B has not used words like 'increase' and 'decrease' to describe the trends — instead the figures are simply stated. It is a common mistake to give a figure such as 160 000 when reading a graph like this with axes that say 'per 100 000'. The candidate should have written that the *death rate* was 160 *per 100 000* (i.e. 160 people for every 100 000 of the population). In fact the *total* number of deaths from malaria in Africa in 1997 was estimated as 960 000 and most of these were of young children who are most susceptible to malaria. Candidate B then attempts to *explain* the trend in Africa, which is not required by the question, and gains no marks.

(Note: If you have to read off figures from a graph then use a ruler.)

Candidate A

(d) Malaria was controlled in many countries by using insecticides to kill mosquitoes and by removing the places where mosquitoes breed. Control programmes were very effective in North America and Mediterranean countries. After about 1970, mosquitoes became resistant to insecticides, and control programmes were less effective, especially in Africa where there were many wars. *Plasmodium* has also become resistant to the drugs used to control it, like chloroquine. As there is no vaccine, it is not possible to give people immunity to malaria.

Candidate B

(d) It is difficult to control mosquitoes in Africa and that is why there are many deaths from the disease there now. Also, there aren't many doctors or hospitals to treat people. The disease has been controlled in the rest of the world and that is why there are few deaths.

> *e* Candidate A gives some *reasons* for the decrease in deaths from malaria in the rest of the world and for the increase in Africa since the middle of the last century. The answer also includes some good detailed knowledge, such as the name of one of the main drugs used to control malaria. If you are asked to 'explain', you should give reasons. When there are several marks (4 in this question) then you should give at least four different points; further detail (e.g. chloroquine in this answer) will often gain marks. Candidate B says that it has proved 'difficult' to control malaria in Africa (no marks) and gives one reason (few hospitals and doctors), which gains a mark, but does not give any more points. The last sentence is too vague for a mark.

Candidate A

(e) Malaria is an ever-changing disease. *Plasmodium* is eukaryotic and has a complex genome with many genes. This means that there are many different strains with different surface antigens. It is not possible to develop a vaccine for all of them.

Candidate B

(e) Some mosquitoes are resistant to the vaccine and once they reproduce there are many more of them. People are also resistant to the drugs that are used to control malaria.

> *e* This question is based on one of the learning outcomes in the immunity section, but is relevant here. Do not expect all the parts of each question to be on the learning outcomes in one section only. Candidate A has given an excellent answer. If you have not read page 45, you may want to turn to that now to find out why. Candidate B has made two common mistakes in answer to this question:
> * Vaccines are developed against pathogens, such as *Plasmodium*; the mosquito is the *vector* of the disease. The candidate should have written 'Mosquitoes have become resistant to insecticides'.
> * People have not become resistant to the drugs; it is the pathogen (*Plasmodium*) which has become resistant.

> *e* **Candidate B gains 2 marks out of 15 for this question.**

Immunity

(a) Below is a list of cells, labelled **A** to **F**, which are involved in defence against disease. Each of the statements numbered **1** to **6** refers to one of these cells. Match a statement to each of these cells.

(A) neutrophil
(B) T helper lymphocyte
(C) macrophage
(D) plasma cell
(E) mast cell
(F) killer T lymphocyte

(1) secretes antibodies
(2) destroys cells infected with viruses
(3) phagocytic cell with lobed nucleus
(4) cell type that is infected by **HIV**
(5) secretes histamine during asthma attacks
(6) phagocytic cell involved in antigen presentation during the immune response

A ...... B ...... C ...... D ...... E ...... F ......   (6 marks)

(b) Explain when it might be appropriate to give someone an injection of antibodies. (2 marks)

The **MMR** vaccine is given to protect children against measles, mumps and rubella between 12 and 15 months of age. Figure 1 shows what happens to the concentration of antibody to measles following vaccination at 12 months.

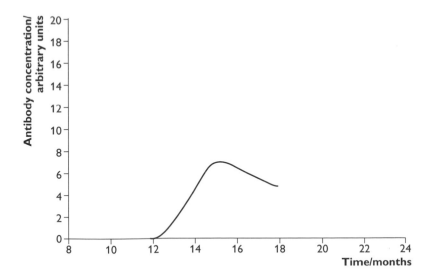

Figure 1

(c) Complete Figure 1 to show what would happen to the concentration of antibody if a vaccinated child was infected with measles at 18 months of age.   (2 marks)

(d) In this question, 1 mark is available for the quality of written communication. Describe the sequence of events that occurs during the first immune response to a vaccine, such as that for measles.   (8 marks)

71

question

(e) Explain why vaccination against one disease, such as measles, does not provide protection against another, such as influenza. (2 marks)

Total: 20 marks

■ ■ ■

Candidates' answers to Question 8

Candidate A

(a) **A** 3; **B** 4; **C** 6; **D** 1; **E** 5; **F** 2

Candidate B

(a) **A** 6; **B** 5; **C** 3; **D** 1; **E** 4; **F** 2

e Candidate B has two correct here, for 2 marks.

Candidate A

(b) To give them passive immunity if they do not have an immune system that responds to pathogens.

Candidate B

(b) The person may have a wound that is infected with tetanus. Tetanus bacteria release a toxic substance that works quickly on the body — the antibodies combine with the toxin, so making it harmless.

e Both candidates have given answers worthy of 2 marks. It is a good idea to give people antibodies against tetanus for the reason given by Candidate B. Injection of antibodies is passive immunity. It is only effective for a short time as the body removes the antibodies and no immune response occurs. There are no memory cells produced when someone is given passive immunity.

Candidate A

(c)

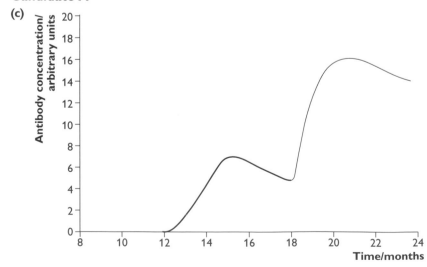

Candidate B

(c)

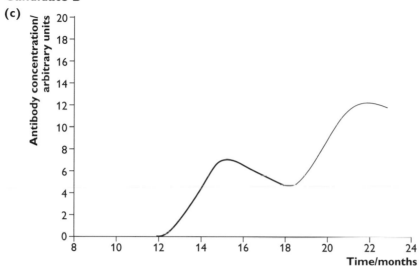

 Adding lines to diagrams or graphs can be difficult. Unlike Candidate A, Candidate B has not made it clear that the secondary immune response is faster than the primary, but does gain 1 mark for showing that a greater concentration of this antibody is produced.

Candidate A

(d) When someone is vaccinated, antigens are 'presented' by macrophages. This means that they expose the antigen on their cell surface membrane. Any T and B lymphocytes with receptors that match the antigen are stimulated to divide. These are cells that are specific to the antigen. T helper cells release molecules that stimulate B cells to divide. B cells divide by mitosis to form plasma cells and memory cells. This stage is clonal expansion. Plasma cells secrete the right type of antibody that fits the antigen. These antibodies go into the blood and go around the body. The amount of this specific antibody increases, as shown in the graph. Memory cells remain in the body ready to respond a second time when the booster is given or when that person becomes infected by measles.

Candidate B

(d) T and B cells respond to the vaccine by producing antibodies. When the antigen is in the body, the B cells divide and begin to make antibiotics. These antibiotics can destroy any pathogen. Memory cells are formed so that when the disease enters the body again there can be more antibiotics formed and you do not get ill. This is why people are given boosters so that they make more antibiotics that give them immunity for life.

 Candidate A has written a well structured and logically presented answer which would gain the mark for quality of written communication. The stages of the immune response are described, although only one of them (clonal expansion) is named. But this does not matter as the answer gives more than the minimum number of marking points available. Candidate B has not written a well structured answer because most of it is concerned with the secondary response which involves memory cells. The candidate has not answered the question. Have you noticed that the candidate has written 'antibiotic' instead of antibody? This is a common error. Antibiotics and antibodies are different and should not be confused. It may just be a 'slip of the pen', but the examiner cannot assume that this is the case. There would be a mark for stating that B cells (or plasma cells) release antibodies but the candidate has said that T and B cells produce antibodies and that is incorrect. No marks can be awarded for this answer.

Candidate A

(e) The antigens on the surfaces of pathogens are different. Only T and B cells specific to measles respond to the measles vaccination. This means that antibodies specific to measles are produced that would not be effective against influenza because it has different-shaped molecules on its surface.

Candidate B

(e) Antibodies produced against measles only fit antigens on the measles viruses. They do not fit on influenza. The shapes of antibodies are important.

    Candidate A has explained the idea of specificity very well. This is a useful word to use when writing about antigens and antibodies. Candidate B has the right idea and gains 1 mark, but 'the shapes of antibodies are important' is vague unless explained with some more detail. The candidates could have referred to the variable regions of antibodies (see Figure 21 on page 42) in their answers.

    Candidate B is awarded 6 marks out of 20 for this question, giving an overall score of 39 marks, which is 33% of the total available. This is just below the mark needed for a grade E. You may have noticed that Candidate B lost marks for many different reasons:

- Some answers are not developed in full, for example Q.3(b) and Q.8(d).
- Appropriate terms are not used, for example Q.4(b) and Q.5(a)(i).
- Terms with similar spellings are confused, for example Q.8(d).
- Terms are spelt incorrectly, for example Q.6(b).
- Calculations are not carried out correctly, for example Q.2(b)(i) and Q.4(a)(iv).
- Instructions are not followed carefully, for example Q.1(d)(i).
- Common errors of understanding are made, for example Q.1(b) and Q.2(e).
- Figures have been misread from graphs, for example Q.7(c).
- Data provided have not been studied carefully, for example Q.6(e).
- Questions have not been read carefully, for example Q.2(f).

These are all examples of poor examination technique. With practice, you can avoid making these errors by reading the examination paper carefully and checking over your answers. With more care, Candidate B could easily gain enough marks to reach grade C or better.